200
HOUSE PLANTS
ANYONE CAN GROW

Richard Gilbert

DORLING KINDERSLEY LONDON

Project Editor   Heather Dewhurst
Art Editor   Fiona Macmillan

Editorial Director   Jackie Douglas
Art Director   Roger Bristow

First published in Great Britain in 1988 by
Dorling Kindersley Limited, London

Copyright © 1988 Dorling Kindersley Limited, London
Text copyright © 1988 Richard Gilbert

British Library Cataloguing in Publication Data

Gilbert, Richard
    200 house plants anyone can grow.
    1. House plants
    I. Title
    635.9'65   SB419

    ISBN 0-86318-276-3

Typeset in Bembo by Chambers Wallace
Printed and bound in Hong Kong

CONTENTS

Introduction

Whether you live in the heart of the country or the middle of a large, sprawling city, house plants will improve the quality of your life. Indoor plants have something not found in the inanimate objects with which people are normally surrounded. A painting or a piece of sculpture may give great and continuing pleasure, but it is static and unchanging. Living plants, on the other hand, have great beauty and they are constantly changing. One day a house plant can appear to be a mass of foliage and then suddenly a flowerbud will appear in the fold of the leaves or at a growing tip and you can watch it develop day by day. Watching leaves unfold or shoots develop can bring great pleasure. Purely from a decorative point of view, a well-grown plant deserves, and usually receives, more than just a passing glance. Having plants at close quarters allows you to admire the texture of their leaves, and to appreciate their subtle leaf patterns and markings, their simplicity of outline, or their more dramatic and unusual shapes. Leaf and flower colour can be subtle and soothing or strong and exhilarating.

Plants in the home

As more and more people move into high-rise apartments whether through necessity or by choice, the need for contact with plants increases. Looking after house plants will give you a link, however tenuous, with nature itself. Having said that, house plants should not be regarded as purely for city people, as substitutes for a proper garden. House plants have their place in every home and are appreciated equally by people who live in the country, surrounded by fields, trees and flowering plants. There is a wide variety of plants to choose from for growing in your home. There are small plants for tabletops and terrariums, trailing plants for hanging baskets, and large stately plants for standing on the floor. Leaf shapes and sizes vary, as do their colours, and there are many plants with decorative and unusual flowers. Obviously your choice will be limited to some extent by the growing conditions available. If your home is very light and airy you will have more choice, though some plants appreciate, and indeed thrive in, shadier conditions.

Plants have different roles to play in a home. Foliage plants form the backbone of most plant collections, giving year-round pleasure and both strong and subtle colour. They certainly need not be dull. Flowering plants perform in a different way; some have a brief, but perhaps glorious, flowering period and then a relatively dull period before they flower again. Some plants such as African violets (*Saintpaulia* hybrids), shrimp plants (*Justicia brandegeana*) and busy Lizzies (*Impatiens wallerana*) can flower continuously for most of the year. Others, such as anthuriums and poinsettias, may not flower continuously but the flower-heads that are produced are very striking and can remain decorative for several months. Poinsettias, for example, often thought of as spectacular ten-day winter wonders, can still be carrying their brightly-coloured bracts in midsummer.

Some colourful flowering plants only flower for a short period and then die, or are very difficult to keep for another year. These are known as temporary flowering house plants. They should be displayed and enjoyed whilst at their best and then discarded.

Elegant arrangement (right)
*A shady corner of a room is enhanced by a simple plant display, featuring a splendid peacock plant (*Calathea makoyana*) offset by two creeping figs (*Ficus pumila*).*

Modern ethnic style (right)
A bright and spacious modern interior provides the ideal setting for this colourful collection of plants. Two Peperomia magnoliifolia *stand in the foreground, backed by a large* Codiaeum variegatum pictum *(in the white pot) and two* Coleus blumei *hybrids. In the background is an impressive* Yucca elephantipes, *softened from above by a trailing* Hedera helix.

How to display plants

At one time, all house plants used to be displayed on a window-sill, regardless of their size, shape or their decorative properties. Now more attention is paid to the look of plants, and their position in the home is more thoughtfully considered. How you display your plants is a matter of personal taste but as with most aspects of design it is often useful to have some guidance. One of the purposes of this book is to point out the potential of plants and suggest ways in which they might be used and displayed effectively. This is not to say, however, that every suggestion should be slavishly copied. For example, aspidistras were beloved of the Victorians but they don't *always* have to be displayed in jardinières on tall pedestals, surrounded by ornaments and backed with plum-red plush; they can look just as effective in a simple or stark modern interior.

Decorative ideas

General guidelines for using plants as decoration can be useful, and there are many ideas given in the book. For instance, large, "architectural" plants, such as many of the tall-growing palms, look best on their own, as a dramatic focal point in a room. Small flowering plants, on the other hand, often benefit if several of them are grown together. For example, try growing several deep

Abundance of greenery
(right)
With the addition of several well-chosen foliage plants, the living room (below) is completely transformed (right).

The effect has been to soften the rather harsh outlines of the room whilst adding to its air of luxury. Colour is provided by a few carefully placed pink and red flowering sinningias.

purple African violets (*Saintpaulia* hybrids) together in a shallow wicker basket for a striking display of colour.

Cool green foliage can humanize an otherwise spartan room, and a grouping of green foliage plants can be used decoratively in several ways. You can make a room divider by grouping large, bushy plants together, or make a curtain of greenery by fitting glass shelves into a window and filling them with small plants, trailing ones as well as bushy ones; this is one way to solve the problem of an unwanted view! Don't limit yourself to window-sills and shelves; a hanging basket planted with colourful trailing tradescantias, for instance, can look very decorative. Most people like to use house plants in a restrained

Dramatic colour *(far right)*
Here the strong reds and greens of Rhoeo spathacea *'Variegata' are echoed by the* Cordyline terminalis *behind. Trailing ivies and a tradescantia add a finishing touch.*

Contrasting shapes *(below)*
This display features (from left to right) an arching Beaucarnea

recurvata, *a bizarre-shaped* Platycerium bifurcatum, *a compact* Aphelandra squarrosa *'Louisae' and a large, bushy* Polypodium aureum.

Pretty display *(right)*
This subtle combination of ferns, begonias, a weeping fig and a syngonium creates an air of softness and delicacy.

Tabletop arrangement
(right)
Several fittonias, marantas and peperomias are grouped together in a wicker basket for a pleasing combination of leaf patterns, colours and textures.

manner, limiting their use in a room to a single plant or only a few well-grown plants, often with telling effect. Other people, however, prefer to create a jungle, where plants are everywhere you look and in no order whatsoever. But whichever plants are chosen and however they are displayed, they should not be allowed to dominate a room and become too overpowering.

Grouping plants together

Plants with differing leaf textures often look good growing in close association: the smooth surface of one plant's leaves will accentuate the ridged or corrugated surface of another's. The white, mealy texture of the frilled-edged leaves of *Cotyledon undulata,* for instance, will contrast dramatically with the glossy, leathery foliage of *Ficus elastica,* while the curving leaves of *Nephrolepis exaltata* will serve to add a crisp, fresh touch.

As with house decorating, use strong colour contrast to make a point or choose only those plants that will blend in with each other to form a harmonious display. There are many house plants that display lovely ranges of foliage colour. *Caladium hortulanum,* for instance, can have spectacular variations of red, pink, white and green leaves, while *Codiaeum variegatum pictum* can present dramatic yellow patterning. In addition to the colour of the foliage, many house plants develop brilliantly coloured flowers, such as *Hippeastrum* hybrids, or, on a smaller scale, the unusual slipper-shaped flowers of *Calceolaria herbeohybrida* hybrids, that can appear in shades of bright yellow or red.

The growing needs of plants should always be considered before grouping plants together. Those plants with variegated leaves must have brighter light than plants with plain green foliage to maintain the sharp colour contrast between the green and the variegation. If insufficient light reaches the plant, the leaves dull and in some cases sections of the plant become totally green.

When mixing plants together in a bowl or trough, remember that some plants like a lot of water whereas others prefer dry conditions: the two cannot really be mixed successfully. Light and temperature needs of the plants must also be considered. You cannot successfully grow a group of plants in bright sunshine, when half of the plants prefer the shade. However, there is one aspect in which grouped plants benefit, and that is humidity. All plants lose moisture into the air and when several plants are grown together the air becomes charged with moisture. Grouped plants usually thrive because of this close association and the increased level of humidity available.

The key to success

Growing house plants, however, is not all a matter of watering, feeding, and providing the correct levels of light, temperature and humidity, although obviously these are important and plants that are well cared for will certainly thrive. The main reason for growing house plants is to *enjoy* them, their shapes and colours, their flowers and foliage, and the way they change and grow from one month to the next. And the purpose of this book is to ensure that you do enjoy them. The 200 house plants featured are all easy to grow, and need only involve the minimum amount of care. By following the simple growing instructions outlined for each plant and by being inspired to display them in effective ways, you will be able to enjoy healthy, thriving house plants all year round.

Plant Finder's Guide

BUSHY FOLIAGE PLANTS

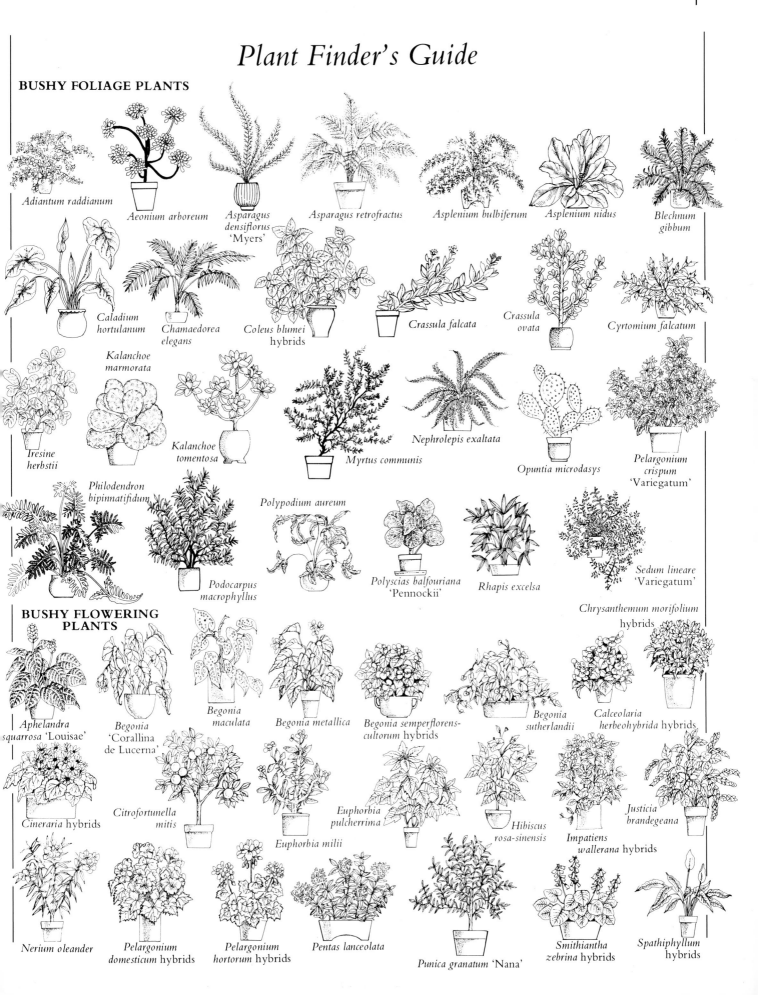

Adiantum raddianum

Aeonium arboreum

Asparagus densiflorus 'Myers'

Asparagus retrofractus

Asplenium bulbiferum

Asplenium nidus

Blechnum gibbum

Caladium hortulanum

Chamaedorea elegans

Coleus blumei hybrids

Crassula falcata

Crassula ovata

Cyrtomium falcatum

Kalanchoe marmorata

Iresine herbstii

Kalanchoe tomentosa

Myrtus communis

Nephrolepis exaltata

Opuntia microdasys

Pelargonium crispum 'Variegatum'

Philodendron bipinnatifidum

Podocarpus macrophyllus

Polypodium aureum

Polyscias balfouriana 'Pennockii'

Rhapis excelsa

Sedum lineare 'Variegatum'

BUSHY FLOWERING PLANTS

Chrysanthemum morifolium hybrids

Aphelandra squarrosa 'Louisae'

Begonia 'Corallina de Lucerna'

Begonia maculata

Begonia metallica

Begonia semperflorens-cultorum hybrids

Begonia sutherlandii

Calceolaria herbeohybrida hybrids

Cineraria hybrids

Citrofortunella mitis

Euphorbia pulcherrima

Euphorbia milii

Hibiscus rosa-sinensis

Impatiens wallerana hybrids

Justicia brandegeana

Nerium oleander

Pelargonium domesticum hybrids

Pelargonium hortorum hybrids

Pentas lanceolata

Punica granatum 'Nana'

Smithiantha zebrina hybrids

Spathiphyllum hybrids

SMALL TABLETOP PLANTS

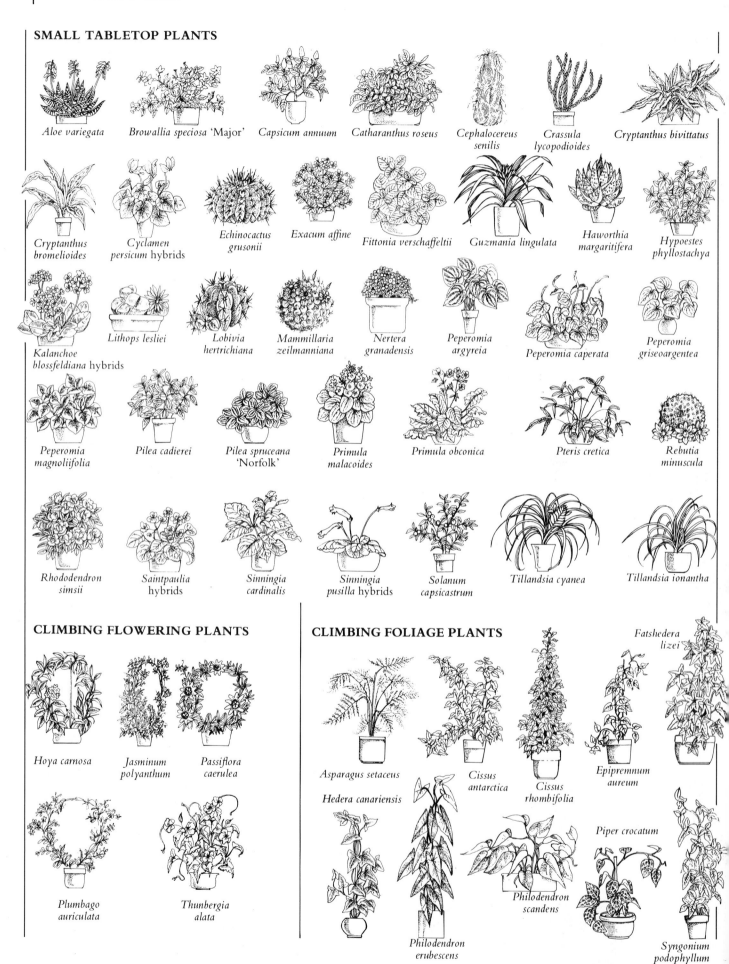

Aloe variegata

Browallia speciosa 'Major'

Capsicum annuum

Catharanthus roseus

Cephalocereus senilis

Crassula lycopodioides

Cryptanthus bivittatus

Cryptanthus bromelioides

Cyclamen persicum hybrids

Echinocactus grusonii

Exacum affine

Fittonia verschaffeltii

Guzmania lingulata

Haworthia margaritifera

Hypoestes phyllostachya

Kalanchoe blossfeldiana hybrids

Lithops lesliei

Lobivia hertrichiana

Mammillaria zeilmanniana

Nertera granadensis

Peperomia argyreia

Peperomia caperata

Peperomia griseoargentea

Peperomia magnoliifolia

Pilea cadierei

Pilea spruceana 'Norfolk'

Primula malacoides

Primula obconica

Pteris cretica

Rebutia minuscula

Rhododendron simsii

Saintpaulia hybrids

Sinningia cardinalis

Sinningia pusilla hybrids

Solanum capsicastrum

Tillandsia cyanea

Tillandsia ionantha

CLIMBING FLOWERING PLANTS

Hoya carnosa

Jasminum polyanthum

Passiflora caerulea

Plumbago auriculata

Thunbergia alata

CLIMBING FOLIAGE PLANTS

Fatshedera lizei

Asparagus setaceus

Hedera canariensis

Cissus antarctica

Cissus rhombifolia

Epipremnum aureum

Piper crocatum

Philodendron scandens

Philodendron erubescens

Syngonium podophyllum

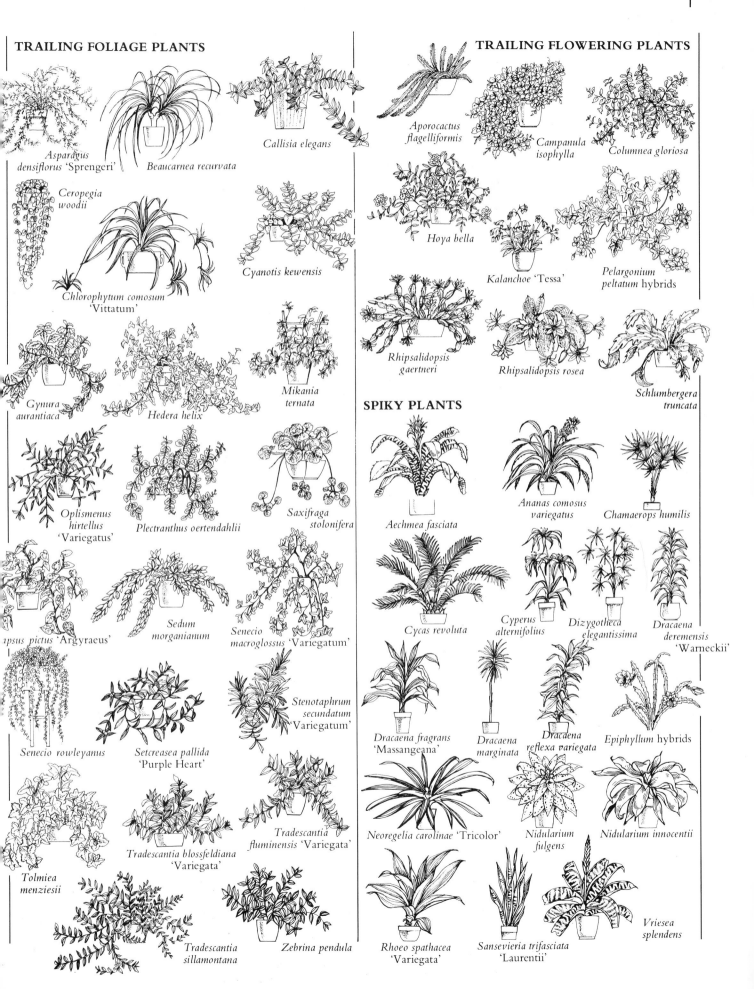

TRAILING FOLIAGE PLANTS

Asparagus densiflorus 'Sprengeri'

Beaucarnea recurvata

Callisia elegans

Ceropegia woodii

Chlorophytum comosum 'Vittatum'

Cyanotis kewensis

Gynura aurantiaca

Hedera helix

Mikania ternata

Oplismenus hirtellus 'Variegatus'

Plectranthus oertendahlii

Saxifraga stolonifera

...psus pictus 'Argyraeus'

Sedum morganianum

Senecio macroglossus 'Variegatum'

Senecio rowleyanus

Setcreasea pallida 'Purple Heart'

Stenotaphrum secundatum 'Variegatum'

Tolmiea menziesii

Tradescantia blossfeldiana 'Variegata'

Tradescantia fluminensis 'Variegata'

Tradescantia sillamontana

Zebrina pendula

TRAILING FLOWERING PLANTS

Aporocactus flagelliformis

Campanula isophylla

Columnea gloriosa

Hoya bella

Kalanchoe 'Tessa'

Pelargonium peltatum hybrids

Rhipsalidopsis gaertneri

Rhipsalidopsis rosea

Schlumbergera truncata

SPIKY PLANTS

Aechmea fasciata

Ananas comosus variegatus

Chamaerops humilis

Cycas revoluta

Cyperus alternifolius

Dizygotheca elegantissima

Dracaena deremensis 'Warneckii'

Dracaena fragrans 'Massangeana'

Dracaena marginata

Dracaena reflexa variegata

Epiphyllum hybrids

Neoregelia carolinae 'Tricolor'

Nidularium fulgens

Nidularium innocentii

Rhoeo spathacea 'Variegata'

Sansevieria trifasciata 'Laurentii'

Vriesea splendens

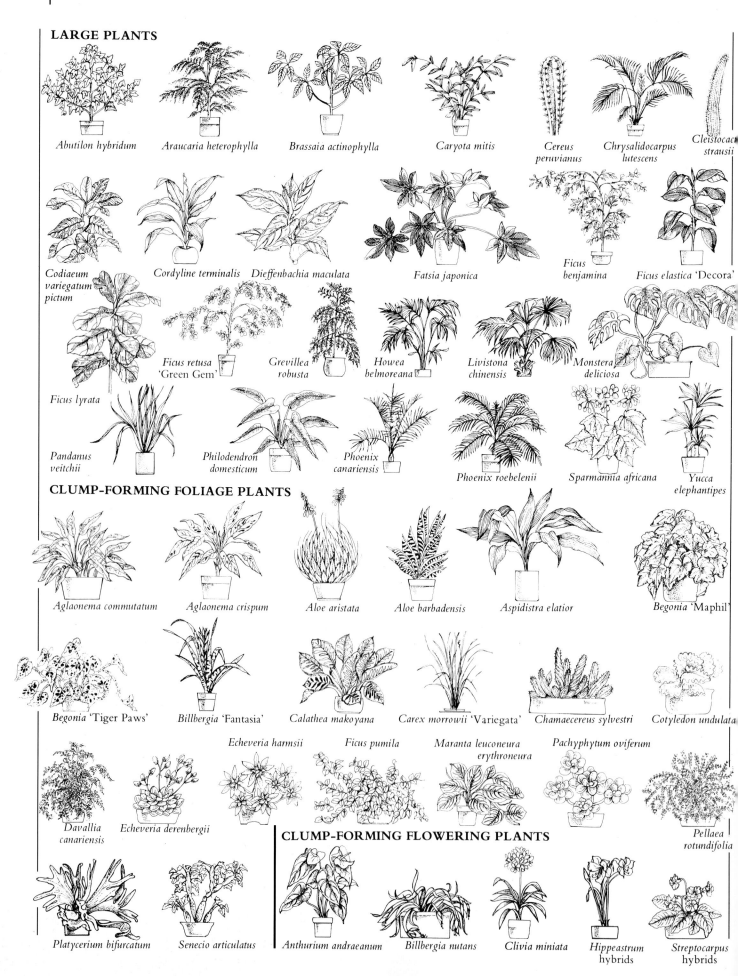

LARGE PLANTS

Abutilon hybridum

Araucaria heterophylla

Brassaia actinophylla

Caryota mitis

Cereus peruvianus

Chrysalidocarpus lutescens

Cleistocac strausii

Codiaeum variegatum pictum

Cordyline terminalis

Dieffenbachia maculata

Fatsia japonica

Ficus benjamina

Ficus elastica 'Decora'

Ficus retusa 'Green Gem'

Grevillea robusta

Howea belmoreana

Livistona chinensis

Monstera deliciosa

Ficus lyrata

Pandanus veitchii

Philodendron domesticum

Phoenix canariensis

Phoenix roebelenii

Sparmannia africana

Yucca elephantipes

CLUMP-FORMING FOLIAGE PLANTS

Aglaonema commutatum

Aglaonema crispum

Aloe aristata

Aloe barbadensis

Aspidistra elatior

Begonia 'Maphil'

Begonia 'Tiger Paws'

Billbergia 'Fantasia'

Calathea makoyana

Carex morrowii 'Variegata'

Chamaecereus sylvestri

Cotyledon undulata

Echeveria harmsii

Ficus pumila

Maranta leuconeura erythroneura

Pachyphytum oviferum

Davallia canariensis

Echeveria derenbergii

Pellaea rotundifolia

CLUMP-FORMING FLOWERING PLANTS

Platycerium bifurcatum

Senecio articulatus

Anthurium andraeanum

Billbergia nutans

Clivia miniata

Hippeastrum hybrids

Streptocarpus hybrids

THE
A-Z
PLANT GUIDE

PLANT CARE SYMBOLS

Light

Medium light An area near a sunless window or 1.5-2 m (4-6 ft) away from a sunny window.

Bright filtered light An area that receives direct sunlight filtered by a blind or curtain.

Direct sunlight A position that receives bright sunshine for most or at least part of the day.

Water

Water sparingly This means barely moistening the potting mixture, and allowing it to dry out almost completely between applications.

Water moderately This means moistening the potting mixture and then allowing the top 2 cm (1 in) to dry out between applications.

Water plentifully This means keeping the potting mixture moist at all times.

Temperature

Cool Plants should ideally be kept at a temperature of between 10-12°C (50-55°F), particularly during the rest period.

Moderate Plants should be kept at a temperature of around 15-18°C (60-65°F).

High Plants should be kept at a temperature of around 18-24°C (65-75°F).

Humidity

Low humidity Plants thrive in dry air.

Moderate humidity Plants prefer extra humidity to be provided.

High humidity Plants need high humidity in order to survive.

1

Abutilon hybridum

FLOWERING MAPLE

This fast-growing shrub can grow to 1.5 m (5 ft) tall, but can be kept shorter with careful pruning (see page 127). The bell-shaped flowers may be white, yellow, orange or red, and they appear in summer and autumn.

Light This plant needs direct sunlight throughout the year.
Water Water moderately and feed with a standard liquid fertilizer every two weeks from early spring to late autumn. Water sparingly during the winter rest period.
Temperature Normal room temperatures are suitable, with at least 10°C (50°F) in winter.
Humidity The flowering maple prefers increased humidity; mist-spray occasionally as this discourages red spider mites.

Decorating tip
Position a large abutilon as a focal point in a sunny window, where the leaves and hanging bell-shaped flowers will be shown off to good advantage in the sunlight.

2

Adiantum raddianum

DELTA MAIDENHAIR

This popular fern grows to around 45 cm (18 in) tall and wide. Its arching fronds carry many small, bright green "leaves" on black stalks. There are also other varieties of adiantum that are more compact or have denser foliage.

Light Grow in medium light from late spring to late autumn, and in bright filtered light in winter.
Water Water a mature plant plentifully during the active growth period. Stand the pot in a deep bowl of water to allow the rootball to become thoroughly moist. Water a younger plant or one that is resting moderately. Feed with a standard liquid fertilizer once a month during the active growth period.

Temperature Normal room temperatures are suitable, with a minimum of 10°C (50°F) in winter.
Humidity High humidity is essential. Stand the pot on a tray of moist pebbles.
Extra point Fronds rarely stay in good condition beyond a year. In spring cut out the older fronds, right back to the base, a few at a time, to allow space for the new fronds to develop and mature.

Decorating tip
The delicate arching fronds of this plant can be displayed to great advantage by placing the pot on a pedestal or tall plant stand.

3

Aechmea fasciata

URN PLANT

The central flower spike of this plant provides decoration for several months, although the actual flowers are short-lived. A rosette of leaves will only flower once, and offsets then appear to replace the parent plant.

Light Grow in direct sunlight.
Water Water moderately, and keep the centre cup topped up with fresh water. Feed with a standard liquid fertilizer once every two weeks during the active growth period.
Temperature Normal room temperatures are suitable.
Humidity This plant prefers increased humidity.

Decorating tip
After the plant has flowered, cut off the old rosette of leaves, leaving the new basal offsets to develop into a striking multi-headed plant. The same effect can be achieved by planting three medium-sized plants in the same container.

4

Aeonium arboreum

The striking feature of this plant is the rosette shape of its tightly packed leaves. A plant can have several rosettes on branching stems. Small flowers are produced in mature rosettes, and after a rosette has flowered once, it then dies.

Light Grow the plant in direct sunlight throughout the year.
Water Water moderately and feed with a standard liquid fertilizer once every two weeks during the active growth period. Water sparingly during winter.
Temperature This plant will thrive in a warm room during the active growth period but prefers a temperature of about 10°C (50°F) during the winter rest period.
Humidity The aeonium is not affected by dry air.

Decorating tip
With its bare stems capped with rosettes of leaves this plant has a gaunt sculptural look and is best displayed on its own against a white or pale background.

5

Aglaonema commutatum

CHINESE EVERGREEN

This popular plant makes a pleasing dome-shaped clump of grey-green leaves. The best variety is *A.c.* 'Treubii', a compact plant whose leaves are streaked with yellow.

Light Provide medium light.
Water Water moderately allowing some drying out of the potting mixture between applications. Feed with a standard liquid fertilizer regularly once every two weeks during the active growth period.
Temperature This aglaonema loves warmth. A minimum temperature of 15°C (60°F) is vital.
Humidity This plant requires high humidity. Stand the pot on a tray filled with moist pebbles.

Decorating tip
Use this plant to brighten up a room that does not receive much sun, or a dull corner such as a hallway where not many other plants will grow.

6

Aglaonema crispum 'Silver Queen'
PAINTED DROP-TONGUE

This aglaonema's leaves are thick and fleshy and coloured greyish-green. The variety *A.c.* 'Silver Queen', which is one of the most decorative available, has dark grey-green leaves that are heavily streaked with patches of silvery-white and cream. As a plant gets older it develops stout, scarred "trunks" that are topped with clusters of up to 10 or 15 leaves.

Light Grow this plant in bright filtered light, avoiding direct sun, throughout the year.

Water Water moderately, letting the potting mixture dry out a little between applications. Feed a well-developed aglaonema with a standard liquid fertilizer every two weeks during the active growth period.
Temperature Keep the plant warm, never allowing the temperature to fall below 15°C (60°F).
Humidity High humidity is essential or the leaf tips and margins turn brown. Stand the pot on a tray of moist pebbles and mist-spray the plant on warm days.

Decorating tip
The very subtle colouring of this plant makes it suitable for mixing with bright, colourful plants such as bromeliads with their striking flower-heads, or Cordyline terminalis with its strong purple-red leaves. All of these plants will thrive in the same humid environment.

7

Aloe aristata
LACE ALOE

The lace aloe produces dense rosettes of leaves, each spotted with raised white spots and tapering to a dry point. Orange flowers appear on the plant in early summer.

Light Grow the plant in direct sunlight throughout the year.
Water Water plentifully and feed with a standard liquid fertilizer once every two weeks during the active growth period. Water sparingly during winter.
Temperature Normal room temperatures are suitable, although it will tolerate a minimum winter temperature of 7°C (45°F).
Humidity The lace aloe is tolerant of dry air and does not require extra humidity to be provided.

Decorating tip
If you leave the offsets to mature on the plant, the lace aloe will develop into a large spreading clump. Grow it in a broad, shallow pan for a hummocked, cushion effect, and in the summer there will be a mass of orange flower-heads blooming above the leaf rosettes.

8

Aloe barbadensis

MEDICINE PLANT

This plant is widely believed to have medicinal properties (particularly for healing burns). The fleshy, green leaves are faintly spotted with white, and its short-lived flowers are yellow.

Light Give the plant direct sunlight.
Water Water plentifully and feed with a standard liquid fertilizer once every two weeks during the active growth period. Water more sparingly in winter.
Temperature Normal room temperatures are preferred during the active growth period, but cooler temperatures are required in winter, with a minimum of 10°C (50°F).
Humidity The medicine plant is tolerant of dry air.

Decorating tip

Allow this plant to grow into a large clump and display it in a sunny window so that the lighting will accentuate the decorative, toothed leaf margins.

9

Aloe variegata

PARTRIDGE-BREASTED ALOE

This is the most popular aloe, with its spiralling leaves arranged in three ranks, and its tubular, coral-pink flowers that appear in late winter and early spring.

Light Grow this plant in bright filtered light.
Water Water plentifully and feed with a standard liquid fertilizer once every two weeks during the active growth period. Water the plant more sparingly in winter.
Temperature Normal room temperatures are ideal from early spring to mid-autumn; thereafter move the plant to a cool position with a temperature at around 12°C (55°F) for a short rest period.
Humidity The aloe tolerates dry air and requires no extra humidity.

Decorating tip

This plant is best appreciated at close quarters. Place it on a desk top or other surface where the soft marbling of the leaves can be clearly seen.

10

Ananas comosus variegatus

VARIEGATED PINEAPPLE

This plant is grown for its yellow striped leaves that flush deep pink when grown in direct sunlight. The plain green-leaved form of this plant is the edible pineapple.

Light Grow the plant in direct sunlight. This will bring out the strong leaf colouration, and encourage the plant to produce flowers and fruit.
Water Water a pineapple plant moderately throughout the year. Feed with a standard liquid fertilizer once every two weeks during the active growth period.
Temperature This plant thrives in high temperatures and dislikes anything below 15°C (60°F).
Humidity High humidity is essential for this plant to thrive. Stand the pot on a tray of moist pebbles and mist-spray the plant frequently.
Extra points This bromeliad, unlike most others, is terrestrial (see page 34), and can therefore be grown in a mixture of equal parts of soil-based potting mixture and coarse peat or leafmould. After a plant produces flowers and fruit the rosette of leaves slowly dies, and offsets appear around the base of the plant.

Decorating tip
This plant has a strong sculptural quality and looks very elegant displayed in a formal classical-shaped urn in a dining room.

11

Anthurium andraeanum

OILCLOTH FLOWER

The most striking feature of this plant is its flower-head, which may be white, pink or, more commonly, bright red. The flower-heads are long lasting and may appear on the plant throughout the year.

Light Grow the plant in medium light but move it to bright filtered light during the winter.
Water Water plentifully and feed once every two weeks during the active growth period. Water moderately in winter.
Temperature This plant prefers warm temperatures of between 18-21°C (65-70°F).
Humidity The anthurium needs high humidity to encourage free flowering. Stand the pot on moist pebbles and mist-spray regularly.

Decorating tip
A large anthurium is best displayed on its own to form a strong and colourful focal point in a room.

12

Aphelandra squarrosa 'Louisae'

ZEBRA PLANT

The aphelandra is a very decorative house plant with its white striped leaves and its striking yellow flower-head. Small flowers are produced but these do not last long. The showy yellow bracts (see page 142), however, last for several weeks. The aphelandra is usually bought when in flower. There are a number of other named varieties of *A. squarrosa*, each with some slight variation in bract colouring or subtlety of leaf striping.

Light Provide bright filtered light during the active growth period and direct sunlight during winter.

Water Water plentifully during the active growth period and sparingly during the normally brief winter rest period. The aphelandra is a greedy plant and needs regular liquid feeds when it is growing. Feed it with a tomato-type liquid fertilizer (see page 133) once every two weeks very early in spring, to encourage the flower spikes to develop, and switch to feeding with a standard liquid fertilizer during the active growth period.

Temperature This plant prefers a warm temperature, about 21°C (70°F), for most of the year, but bring the temperature down to around 12°C (55°F) immediately after the plant has flowered, to encourage a rest period.

Humidity This plant thrives in high humidity. Stand the pot on a tray of moist pebbles and mist-spray the foliage on warm days.

Mist-spraying an aphelandra to maintain high humidity

Decorating tip
For an attractive arrangement, group three or more young, well-budded zebra plants together in a simple white bowl or tureen. Leave them in their pots and pack the gaps firmly between the pots with moist peat. Such a display should carry attractive flower-heads for two to three months, and decorative striped leaves for up to six months.

13

Aporocactus flagelliformis

RAT'S TAIL CACTUS

This cactus has prickly trailing stems and produces crimson-pink flowers.

Light Grow in direct sunlight.
Water Water plentifully and feed with a tomato-type liquid fertilizer (see page 133) once every two weeks from early spring to late autumn. Water very sparingly in winter.
Temperature Normal room temperatures are suitable, with a winter rest at 7-10°C (45-50°F).
Humidity This plant likes dry air.

Decorating tip
Grow this cactus in a hanging basket in a sunny window or on a high shelf, where its trailing stems cannot be brushed against.

14

Araucaria heterophylla

NORFOLK ISLAND PINE

The araucaria grows slowly but can reach 120 cm (4 ft) in 10 years.

Light Grow in medium light.
Water Water plentifully and feed with a standard liquid fertilizer once every two weeks during the active growth period. Water moderately during the winter.
Temperature The araucaria does well at 15-21°C (60-70°F).
Humidity This plant prefers increased humidity.

Decorating tip
The araucaria has a very distinctive, stark shape and is best displayed on its own. It is ideal for brightening a dull corner.

15

Asparagus densiflorus 'Myers'

FOXTAIL FERN

This decorative asparagus has plume-like branches, each densely packed with fine green "needles".

Light Grow in bright filtered light.
Water Water plentifully and feed with a standard liquid fertilizer once every two weeks from spring to mid-autumn. Water sparingly during winter.
Temperature Normal room temperatures are suitable, with a winter minimum of 12°C (55°F).
Humidity This plant prefers extra humidity in a warm room. Stand the pot on a tray of moist pebbles.
Extra point The plant's thickened roots will fill out the potting mixture, so leave space for this when repotting the plant (see page 134).

Decorating tip
The arching stems of this asparagus can be displayed by growing the plant in a classical urn-shaped container, with fronds rising upwards and outwards.

16

Asparagus densiflorus 'Sprengeri'

EMERALD FERN

This plant is grown for its attractive, frothy green foliage.

Light Grow the plant in bright filtered light at all times.
Water Water plentifully and feed with a standard liquid fertilizer once every two weeks during the active growth period. Water sparingly during the winter.
Temperature This plant grows well in normal room temperatures and will tolerate a minimum of 12°C (55°F).
Humidity The asparagus prefers extra humidity; mist-spray it if the temperature rises above 18°C (65°F).
Extra point This plant develops fat root sections that can crowd the potting mixture and force it upwards, so leave plenty of space for this when repotting (see page 134).

Decorating tip
Grow the asparagus in a well-lit window in a hanging basket, where the sunlight will emphasize the feathery detail.

17

Asparagus retrofractus

TREE ASPARAGUS

The fine needle-like leaves of this asparagus are arranged in clusters. The stems can be supported by thin canes, or they can be allowed to trail.

Light Give the plant bright filtered light throughout the year.
Water Water plentifully and feed regularly with a standard liquid fertilizer once every two weeks during the active growth period. Water sparingly in winter.
Temperature This plant tolerates normal room temperatures, but prefers a cooler temperature of around 12°C (55°F) in winter.
Humidity This asparagus prefers extra humidity if being grown in a warm room. Stand the pot on a tray of moist pebbles.

Decorating tip
Grow this asparagus with other plants in a large container or trough, where it will add a light frothy touch to the display and its trailing stems will help to soften the hard edges of the trough.

18

Asparagus setaceus

ASPARAGUS FERN

The asparagus fern has thin flattened branches that give it a bushy appearance when it is young, but, as it matures, climbing stems up to 120 cm (4 ft) long start to appear.

Light Grow the asparagus fern in bright filtered light, avoiding hot summer sun, throughout the year.
Water Water plentifully and feed with a standard liquid fertilizer once every two weeks from early spring to mid-autumn. Water sparingly during the winter rest period.
Temperature The asparagus fern enjoys normal room temperatures and will survive happily at 12°C (55°F).
Humidity The plant is tolerant of dry air but prefers extra humidity if the room temperature exceeds 18°C (65°F). Stand the pot on a tray of moist pebbles to increase the humidity.

Decorating tip
Grow an asparagus fern up the frame of an east- or west-facing window, where its delicate frond-like branches will provide a soft edging to the window frame, whilst still allowing plenty of light to enter the room.

19

Aspidistra elatior

CAST-IRON PLANT

The aspidistra is tolerant of some neglect, but, if treated well, will produce several new leaves each year.

Light This plant does best in bright filtered light but will grow in a poorly-lit position for short periods.
Water Water moderately throughout the year. Feed with a standard liquid fertilizer once every two weeks during the active growth period.
Temperature An aspidistra is tolerant of a wide range of temperatures, with a winter minimum of 10°C (50°F).
Humidity The aspidistra needs high humidity.

> **Decorating tip**
> *The aspidistra was one of the few indoor plants to survive gas lighting in Victorian times and, as such, was commonly grown. To give an aspidistra the full "Victorian treatment" today, display it in a cache pot on a pedestal.*

20

Asplenium bulbiferum

HEN-AND-CHICKEN FERN

This fern gets its common name from the way it carries small "offspring" on its fronds, that can be picked off and grown on to become new plants.

Light The plant needs bright filtered light, avoiding direct sun, for its fronds to develop.
Water Water plentifully and feed with a standard liquid fertilizer every two weeks during the active growth period. Water sparingly in winter.
Temperature This plant is tolerant of a wide range of temperatures, with a winter minimum of 10°C (50°F).
Humidity This fern prefers increased humidity or the frond tips go brown. Stand it on moist pebbles.

> **Decorating tip**
> *With its finely divided fronds the hen-and-chicken fern will add contrast to a mixed group of stronger shaped plants.*

21

Asplenium nidus

BIRD'S NEST FERN

The bird's nest fern is a popular house plant and very easy to grow. Its shiny undivided fronds are arranged in a rosette shape, reminiscent of a bird's nest, hence its common name. The texture of its fronds is leathery and the colour a fresh apple green. They can reach 1 m (3-4 ft) long but 35-50 cm (15-18 in) is more common. New, unfurling fronds are rather fragile and easily damaged, and should not be handled for the first few weeks.

Light Give the plant bright filtered light throughout the year, avoiding the hot summer sun.

Water Water plentifully and feed with a standard liquid fertilizer every two weeks during the active growth period. Water sparingly in winter.

Temperature This fern grows well in normal room temperatures, but a minimum of 15°C (60°F) in winter is preferred, for the fronds to remain healthy.

Humidity High humidity is essential to avoid brown leaf tips and edges. Stand the fern on a large tray filled with moist pebbles. Mist-spray the plant regularly to wash off any surface dust, and wipe mature fronds with a damp sponge occasionally.

Repotting an asplenium
You may have to break the pot in order to remove the plant, as its roots will cling to the pot sides.

Decorating tip
A large specimen asplenium looks distinctive on its own. Stand it on a low table or other surface, where its cup-shaped centre can be viewed from above.

Extra points This fern does not produce offsets, the plant simply grows larger. As the plant grows, a strange spongy root mass develops, and slowly spreads over the surface of the potting mixture. This is a signal that the fern needs moving on into a larger pot. Repot in spring, using a rich but free-draining mixture incorporating leafmould or coarse peat.

Problems Watch out for scale insects that can collect on the undersides of the fronds, usually close to the prominent midrib. Check that the pesticide you use is suitable for ferns.

22

Beaucarnea recurvata

PONYTAIL PLANT

The thin arching leaves of this plant grow from a thick corky base. This may be bulb-sized when young but it can grow very big with age.

Light The ponytail plant comes from the dry parts of Mexico and needs to be grown in direct sunlight.
Water Water plentifully and feed with a standard liquid fertilizer once every two weeks from early spring through to mid-autumn. Water *very* sparingly during winter.
Temperature This plant prefers high temperatures during the active growth period but must have a minimum of 10°C (50°F) during the winter.
Humidity The ponytail plant thrives in low humidity.

> **Decorating tip**
> *This unusual plant is ideal for a modern interior, and a well-developed plant looks stunning when displayed on its own, where the marked contrast between the chunky base and the gently arching leaves can be appreciated.*

23

Begonia 'Corallina de Lucerna'

This tall-growing begonia produces large clusters of rose-red flowers during winter and spring.

Light Grow in direct sunlight.
Water Water moderately. Feed an established plant with a standard liquid fertilizer once every two weeks during the active growth period.
Temperature Normal room temperatures are suitable with a winter minimum of 12°C (55°F).
Humidity This begonia is tolerant of dry air, but prefers increased humidity in a high temperature.

> **Decorating tip**
> *A tall plant makes a striking feature when it flowers, as several dense heads of drooping blooms will appear on each stem and continue flowering for three to four months. Stand the plant in a sunny room and tie its stems loosely to supports or the heavy trusses of flowers might snap them.*

24

Begonia maculata

This begonia has dark green leaves that are heavily spotted with silver. Its flowers are small, very pale pink, and they appear throughout the year.

Light Grow the plant in bright filtered light throughout the year.
Water Water moderately and feed with a standard liquid fertilizer once every two weeks from early spring to mid-autumn. Water more sparingly during the winter.
Temperature Normal room temperatures are suitable for this begonia, with a minimum during winter of 12°C (55° F).
Humidity This plant is not demanding in this respect, but it prefers increased humidity when the room temperature rises.

> **Decorating tip**
> *This begonia can be used to add interest to a group of mixed plants, as its silvery-spotted leaves contrast well with plants that have plainer foliage. It can also add height to such a mixed planting.*

25

Begonia 'Maphil'

Sometimes known as *B.* 'Cleopatra', *B.* 'Maphil' is perhaps the best known rhizomatous begonia (see page 142) ever to have been introduced. Its star-shaped leaves are variable in colour (depending on the light intensity) but usually they are a rusty-gold with green and brown markings. Bristly hairs sprout from the leaf edges.

Light Grow the plant in bright filtered light throughout the year. Winter sunshine will not harm it.
Water Water moderately and feed with a standard liquid fertilizer once every two weeks during the active growth period. Water sparingly during winter.
Temperature Normal room temperatures are suitable for this begonia, but it prefers a cooler winter rest period at around 15°C (60°F).
Humidity This plant prefers increased humidity. Stand the pot on a generous-sized tray filled with moist pebbles and mist-spray the plant regularly.
Propagation *B.* 'Maphil' can be increased by leaf cuttings. Plant a single leaf in a small pot filled with a mixture of equal parts of moist peat and coarse sand or perlite. Cover the pot with a plastic bag to conserve moisture and keep it in bright filtered light in a warm place until the new plantlets appear.

Decorating tip
Plant up a 25-30 cm (10-12 in) hanging basket with three or four well-rooted cuttings of B. 'Maphil' in early spring. By the following spring, the basket will look very showy, with 20-30 cm (8-12 in) tall flower spikes carrying a mass of small, pale pink flowers.

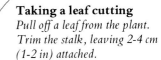

Taking a leaf cutting
Pull off a leaf from the plant. Trim the stalk, leaving 2-4 cm (1-2 in) attached.

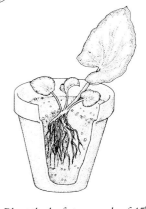

Plant the leaf at an angle of 45° in a pot of moist peat and coarse sand. New plantlets soon grow.

26

Begonia metallica

METALLIC-LEAF BEGONIA

This shrubby, hairy-leaved begonia produces pale pink flowers, bearded with pink bristly hairs, during summer.

Light Grow the plant in bright filtered light.
Water Water moderately and feed with a standard liquid fertilizer once every two weeks during the active growth period. Water sparingly during winter.
Temperature Normal room temperatures are suitable.
Humidity This plant prefers increased humidity if being grown in a warm room.
Extra point This begonia can be increased by stem cuttings (see page 136) but make sure that the rooting mixture is only just moist (never wet) or they will rot.

Decorating tip
A most effective way to display this begonia is to stand it in a bright window, where the striking deep purple colouring of its foliage can be seen more clearly.

27

Begonia semperflorens-cultorum hybrids

WAX BEGONIA

This very popular begonia has white, pink or red flowers and its leaves are fleshy and coloured green or brown.

Light Grow the plant in bright filtered light.
Water Water moderately and feed with a standard liquid fertilizer once every two weeks during the active growth period. Water sparingly in winter.
Temperature Normal room temperatures are suitable.
Humidity This plant prefers increased humidity if being grown in a warm room.

Decorating tip
Grow a few wax begonias together in a terracotta trough for a lovely splash of colour, lasting up to four months.

28

Begonia sutherlandii

This low-growing begonia produces small, yellowish-orange flowers from early summer until autumn.

Light Grow the plant in bright filtered light.
Water Water moderately and feed with a standard liquid fertilizer once a month during the active growth period. Stop watering in late autumn.
Temperature Normal room temperatures are suitable for this begonia during the active growth period, but the plant requires a cool winter rest at around 12°C (55°F).
Humidity This plant prefers extra humidity. Stand the pot on a tray of moist pebbles.
Extra point This begonia dies down in late autumn. Leave the tuber dry in its pot until early spring and then repot into fresh potting mixture and treat as above.

Decorating tip
This is an ideal plant to display in a small hanging basket, where its delicate, trailing red stems and fresh green, maple-shaped leaves prove a perfect foil for its many small yellowish-orange flowers.

29

Begonia 'Tiger Paws'

EYELASH BEGONIA

The emerald green leaves of *B.* 'Tiger Paws' are marked with brown and have a bristly "eyelash" edging.

Light Grow the plant in bright filtered light, but keep it out of the hot summer sun.
Water Water moderately and feed with a standard liquid fertilizer once every two weeks during the active growth period. Water sparingly during the winter.
Temperature This begonia grows well in normal room temperatures but likes a cooler rest period, with a minimum of 12°C (55°F).
Humidity This plant prefers extra humidity. Stand the pot on moist pebbles, and mist-spray regularly.

Decorating tip
Grow this plant in a shallow container and stand it on a low table or window ledge where you can look down on the attractive foliage. B. 'Tiger Paws' will spread over the potting mixture and eventually down the sides of the container.

30

Billbergia 'Fantasia'

The leaves of this plant are heavily spotted with cream, and in bright light the whole plant is suffused with a rose-pink colour.

Light Grow in direct sunlight.
Water Water moderately throughout the year. Keep the cup-like centre filled with fresh water (clean rainwater if possible). Feed with a standard liquid fertilizer once every two weeks during the active growth period.
Temperature Normal room temperatures are suitable with a minimum of 12°C (55°F).
Humidity This plant tolerates dry air. Mist-spray occasionally.

Decorating tip
This funnel-shaped plant with its unusual and subtle colouring is best displayed on its own. Stand it under a table lamp so that when it blooms you can see the striking flower-head develop.

31

Billbergia nutans

QUEEN'S-TEARS

Decorating tip
Display this billbergia on a sunny window-sill and allow it to grow into a large clump, when you will be rewarded with a lovely, colourful display of flower spikes with their attendant pink bracts.

This plant develops large clumps of olive-green leaves that turn red in strong sunlight. As with most bromeliads, although the actual flowers are short-lived, the flower spike remains decorative for several months.

Light Grow in very bright light, with at least three hours of direct sunlight a day.

Water Water moderately throughout the year. Keep the cup-like centre of the rosette of leaves filled with fresh water (clean rainwater if possible). Feed with a standard liquid fertilizer once every two weeks during the active growth period.

Temperature This billbergia prefers a temperature at around 15-20°C (60-70°F).

Humidity This plant prefers extra humidity; mist-spray occasionally.

32

Blechnum gibbum

The fronds of this tropical fern, which may be up to 1 m (3 ft) long, grow in an open rosette shape. With age the plant develops a short, black trunk.

Light Grow this fern in bright filtered light.

Water Water plentifully and feed with a standard liquid fertilizer once a month during the active growth period. Water moderately during winter.

Temperature This fern will thrive in normal room temperatures with a winter minimum of 12°C (55°F).

Humidity This fern is more tolerant of dry rooms than most ferns, but in a warm room, place the pot on a tray of moist pebbles for extra humidity.

Decorating tip
A plant that has begun to develop its distinctive trunk makes a strong feature. Stand it on the floor near a window.

33

Brassaia actinophylla

UMBRELLA TREE

The size of the hand-shaped leaves and leaflets of this Australian shrub vary considerably. Young plants usually have two to five leaflets, each around 15 cm (6 in) long; more mature plants can produce up to sixteen leaflets, each around 30 cm (1 ft) long.

Light Grow the umbrella tree in bright filtered light.
Water Water moderately, allowing some drying out of the potting mixture between applications, and feed with a standard liquid fertilizer once every two weeks during the active growth period. Water sparingly in winter.
Temperature The umbrella tree will grow well in normal room temperatures, with a minimum temperature in winter of 12°C (55°F).
Humidity High humidity is essential. Stand the pot on a large tray filled with moist pebbles.
Extra point To keep the large brassaia leaves free from dust, clean them regularly every two weeks with a damp sponge. Support the leaves with one hand whilst cleaning them carefully with the other.

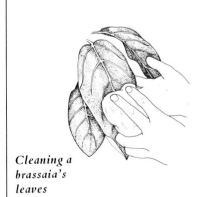

Cleaning a brassaia's leaves

Decorating tip
Its shiny leaves give the umbrella plant a strong, clean look which can be further emphasized by displaying the plant in a cool, modern setting. For added effect, arrange a few interestingly-shaped stones or perhaps a chunk of driftwood around the pebbles of the moisture tray.

BROMELIADS

Bromeliads come mainly from central and South America. Some grow in arid desert-like conditions, whilst others live in the moist tropical rainforests. Most bromeliads are *epiphytes,* which means that they anchor themselves to the trunks and limbs of trees with short, wiry roots and live off what they can take from the air, and the debris that collects in crevices of branches. But other bromeliads are *terrestrial,* which means that they grow in the ground, much like most plants.

All bromeliads are stemless and have a rosette of leaves that may be loose or so tightly arranged that it is capable of holding a reservoir of water the plant can draw on. This habit of holding water is very unusual, and few other plants can tolerate having their growing point submerged. Bromeliads are also able to take moisture from the air with water-absorbent scales (these often look like meal or scurf) on the leaves.

The flower-heads of bromeliads are often striking, and sometimes bizarre; some are backed with brilliantly coloured bracts. They come in all shapes and sizes: "drumsticks", lance- or sword-shaped or broadly branching on long stout stalks, or stemless with the flowers peeping just above water level deep in the central cup-like reservoir. The actual flowers are normally short-lived but the decorative flower-heads are long-lasting. Some

198
Vriesea splendens
Flaming sword

3
Aechmea fasciata
Urn plant

98
Guzmania lingulata
Scarlet star

125
Neoregelia carolinae 'Tricolor'
Blushing bromeliad

develop fruits or berries after flowering. Once a rosette of leaves has produced a flower-head it dies. This may be a very slow process. Offsets form around the base of the plant and these can be used in propagation.

Cultivation
Most bromeliads do well in bright filtered light and warm temperatures. They need to be watered frequently and those with a cup-like centre to the leaves should be topped up with water. Bromeliads prefer a free-draining potting mixture; use peat as a base and then add coarse leafmould, bark chippings, perlite or grit. Feed bromeliads periodically during the active growth period. Always allow the offsets to develop into the characteristic rosette shape before removing them from the parent plant, otherwise they prove difficult to root.

10
Ananas comosus variegatus
Variegated pineapple

31
Billbergia nutans
Queen's-tears

67
Cryptanthus bivittatus

68
Cryptanthus bromelioides 'Tricolor'
Rainbow star

130
Nidularium innocentii
Bird's nest bromeliad

192
Tillandsia cyanea
Blue-flowered torch

193
Tillandsia ionantha

129
Nidularium fulgens

30
Billbergia 'Fantasia'

34

Browallia speciosa 'Major'

SAPPHIRE FLOWER

The violet-blue flowers of the browallia can be up to 4 cm (2 in) across. There are also white-flowered and miniature forms and all flower from midsummer onwards. The browallia is normally treated as a temporary house plant (see page 142) and thrown away when its flowers die.

Light Grow the plant in bright filtered light and when possible a few hours of direct sunlight. With enough bright light a plant will go on flowering into the winter.
Water Water moderately at all times. Feed with a standard liquid fertilizer once every two weeks during the active growth period.
Temperature Grow the plant at about 12-18°C (55-65°F).
Humidity This plant is tolerant of relatively dry air.

Decorating tip

Plant a few browallia plants in a hanging basket, where their thin stems, if unsupported, will cascade over the sides.

35

Caladium hortulanum

ANGEL-WINGS

The decorative, flimsy leaves of this plant can be red, green and cream. The leaves die down in winter.

Light Grow in bright filtered light.
Water Water moderately while the leaves of the plant are decorative. In late autumn, gradually stop watering to allow the leaves to die down and keep the plant dry over the winter. Feed with a standard liquid fertilizer once every two weeks during the active growth period.

Temperature Provide temperatures at around 18-24°C (65-75°F) from spring to autumn. Keep the dry tuber at around 15°C (60°F) in winter.
Humidity This plant prefers extra humidity on hot days.

Decorating tip

With its delicate leaves in their spectacular colours, the caladium is best displayed amongst green-leaved plants, such as Ficus elastica *and* Asplenium nidus.

36

Calathea makoyana

PEACOCK PLANT

The beautifully-marked leaves of the peacock plant grow on long leaf stalks, often in an almost vertical way, which helps to display the patterning on their undersides.

Light Grow the peacock plant in medium light.
Water Water plentifully and feed with a standard liquid fertilizer once every two weeks during the active growth period. Water moderately during the winter.
Temperature Grow the plant at a temperature between 15-21°C (60-70°F) throughout the year.
Humidity High humidity is essential. Stand the pot on a tray of moist pebbles, and mist-spray the plant frequently, ideally with clean rainwater.

Decorating tip
An ideal place to display the peacock plant is an entrance hall, where the light is not too bright to harm the plant, but light enough to show the subtly coloured leaves.

37

Calceolaria herbeohybrida hybrids

SLIPPER FLOWER

This temporary flowering house plant (see page 142) has ballooned flowers that appear in large clusters.

Light Grow this plant in bright filtered light.
Water Water plentifully by soaking the pot and rootball in a deep bowl of water. Feed with a standard liquid fertilizer once every two weeks.
Temperature This plant prefers a cool temperature.
Humidity The slipper flower prefers extra humidity, but do not mist-spray as this can cause rot.

Decorating tip
Group several of these striking plants together in a simple wicker basket to provide a focal point in the room.

38

Callisia elegans
STRIPED INCH PLANT

The leaf striping of this callisia is neater and more striking than that of the variegated-leaved tradescantias, which are close relatives.

Light Grow this callisia in direct sunlight.
Water Water plentifully and feed with a standard liquid fertilizer once every two weeks from early spring to late autumn. Water sparingly during the winter.
Temperature Grow the plant in a warm room for most of the year but give it a winter rest at 12-15°C (55-60°F).
Humidity This plant prefers increased humidity if temperatures soar much above 21°C (70°F).

Decorating tip
The distinctive striping of these leaves should be viewed at close quarters. Grow the plant in a pan or half-pot and place it at a low level, such as on a table under a lamp.

39

Campanula isophylla
STAR-OF-BETHLEHEM

This plant produces very pale blue or white flowers on the tips of trailing stems from midsummer to late autumn.

Light Grow this plant in direct sunlight.
Water Water plentifully and feed with a standard liquid fertilizer once every two weeks during the active growth period. Water sparingly in the winter.
Temperature Grow in a temperature at around 18°C (65°F) for most of the year, and around 7°C (45°F) during the winter.
Humidity This plant needs high humidity.

Decorating tip
Grow a few campanulas in a hanging basket. This will produce a mass of flowers over eight to ten weeks.

40

41

42

Capsicum annuum

CHRISTMAS PEPPER

The capsicum bears fruit that can be round, cone-shaped or acutely pointed. Fruit colour ranges from green, yellow, orange and red to deep purple. This plant should be treated as a temporary plant (see page 142) and discarded when the fruit shrivels.

Light Grow in direct sunlight.
Water Water plentifully and feed with a standard liquid fertilizer once every two weeks.
Temperature A cool temperature will extend the life of this plant. Avoid placing the plant near to a radiator.
Humidity This plant needs high humidity. Stand the pot on a tray filled with moist pebbles.

Decorating tip
With its brightly coloured fruit and glossy green leaves, this ornamental pepper makes an ideal Christmas decoration. Group three or four capsicums together on a table top for a festive display.

Carex morrowii 'Variegata'

JAPANESE SEDGE GRASS

Japanese sedge grass quickly forms dense clumps of grass-like leaves, that can grow to 30 cm (1 ft) tall.

Light Grow the plant in bright filtered light all year.
Water Water moderately at all times. Although Japanese sedge grass is a bogside plant (see page 142), it prefers a potting mixture that dries out a little before the next watering. Feed with a standard liquid fertilizer once every two weeks during the active growth period.
Temperature Japanese sedge grass is tolerant of a wide range of temperatures with a winter minimum of 10°C (50°F).
Humidity High humidity is essential. Stand the pot on moist pebbles.

Decorating tip
Grow Japanese sedge grass alongside other waterside plants such as Cyperus alternifolius, *in a bathroom, where it will also appreciate the high level of humidity.*

Caryota mitis

FISHTAIL PALM

This slow-growing palm has gracefully arching fronds on long leaf stalks. The unusual fishtail-like frond sections are very decorative.

Light Grow the plant in bright filtered light. Move it to a sunny window for the winter.
Water Water plentifully and feed with a standard liquid fertilizer once every two weeks from early spring to mid-autumn. Water moderately during the winter.
Temperature The fishtail palm loves warmth, and will deteriorate quickly at temperatures under 12°C (55°F).
Humidity Stand the pot on a tray of moist pebbles to raise the humidity level. High humidity is essential to keep the frond sections healthy.

Decorating tip
Grow the fishtail palm as a specimen plant in a well-lit window. Against the light, the wedge-shaped frond sections and the arching growth can be fully appreciated.

43

Catharanthus roseus

MADAGASCAR PERIWINKLE

The catharanthus can be bought in flower in mid-spring and continues to bloom well into autumn. Flowers may be white with a strong carmine-red centre, a soft pink or a strong mauve.

Light Grow the plant in bright light, including a few hours of direct sunlight a day if possible.
Water Water plentifully throughout the year. Feed with a standard liquid fertilizer once every two weeks during the flowering period.
Temperature Normal room temperatures are suitable.
Humidity The catharanthus is tolerant of dry air.

Decorating tip
Group several of these plants together in a plain dish or simple basket. Strong pink and mauve-flowered catharanthuses make for a vibrant splash of colour, while the addition of the odd white-flowered plant will tone down the display.

44

Cephalocereus senilis

OLD MAN CACTUS

The striking feature of this cactus is the white hair that all but obscures its columnar body and sharp spines.

Light Grow the plant in direct sunlight. The hairs protect the plant from strong sun, and the stronger the light, the denser are the hairs.
Water Water moderately and feed with a standard liquid fertilizer once every two weeks from early spring to mid-autumn. Water sparingly during winter. In low temperatures, do not water at all.
Temperature This plant enjoys high temperatures but is best kept at around 12°C (55°F) during winter.
Humidity The old man cactus prefers dry air.

Decorating tip
Grow this unusual looking plant on a sunny window-sill with a smooth-skinned succulent, such as Cotyledon undulata, for an interesting contrast of textures.

45

Cereus peruvianus

PERUVIAN APPLE CACTUS

This impressive column-shaped cactus can grow up to 60 cm (2 ft) tall. Flowers are not produced on plants indoors.

Light Grow this plant in direct sunlight. Turn the pot regularly to discourage lopsided growth.
Water Water moderately and feed with a standard liquid fertilizer once every two weeks during the active growth period. Water sparingly during the winter.
Temperature Normal room temperatures are suitable during the active growth period, but move the plant to a cooler position, at around 10°C (50°F), in winter.
Humidity This cactus is tolerant of dry air and needs no extra humidity.
Extra point The cereus can stand outside in the garden in the summer, in a sheltered but sunny position, but it must gradually be accustomed to the brighter light or its leaves will become "scorched".

Decorating tip
This plant is best displayed in a mixed arrangement of cacti and succulents, where its shape and height will contrast well with the other plants.

46

Ceropegia woodii

ROSARY VINE

Small, fleshy heart-shaped leaves with a strong marbled pattern above and pinkish-purple underneath grow from this plant's thread-like stems. Tubular purple flowers appear amongst the leaves from late summer until mid-autumn. The stems are usually allowed to trail over the edge of the pot, but they can be trained upwards on a small bamboo trellis pushed into the potting mixture. The base of the plant is a corky tuber that sits on the surface of the potting mixture. Small tubers grow at irregular intervals along the stems. These can be picked off very easily and then used in propagation.

Light This South African plant needs all the sunshine it can get. Grow it in direct sunlight. Insufficient light results in poor leaf colouring and leggy growth.
Water Water sparingly and feed with a standard liquid fertilizer once a month during the active growth period. Water very sparingly (almost to the point of not at all) during the winter.
Temperature Normal room temperatures throughout the year are suitable for this plant.
Humidity The ceropegia tolerates dry air and does not require extra humidity to be provided.
Extra point To increase plants, remove the small tubers that develop along the stems, and place these on the surface of a pot containing soil-based potting mixture topped with a 1 cm ($\frac{1}{2}$ in) layer of coarse sand or perlite. The tubers should rest on the surface of the potting mixture. They will first send down moisture-seeking roots and later produce new trailing stems.

Decorating tip
Plant several small ceropegias in well-drained potting mixture in a hanging basket and position this in a sunny window. The decorative, marbled leaves and purple flowers can then be fully appreciated.

47

Chamaecereus sylvestri

PEANUT CACTUS

The peanut cactus is very easy to grow and very rewarding. It produces a small clump of spiralled stems, rarely taller than 15 cm (6 in) high, and in summer deep scarlet flowers appear over a period of several weeks.

Light Grow this plant in direct sunlight throughout the year.
Water Water moderately and feed with a standard liquid fertilizer once every two weeks from spring to autumn. Water only sparingly during the winter rest period.
Temperature Normal room temperatures are suitable for this plant during the active growth period, but it requires a cool winter rest with a temperature of about 7°C (45°F).
Humidity The peanut cactus is tolerant of dry air and does not require extra humidity.

Decorating tip
This plant is excellent for displaying on a kitchen window-sill in bright sun. As it is so easy to grow, and grows very quickly, it will provide constant interest.

48

Chamaedorea elegans

PARLOUR PALM

The parlour palm is very easy to grow, and a useful size, not normally growing taller than 120 cm (4 ft) high. Plants can be bought in all sizes, ranging from tiny seedlings, for using in terrariums, to 60-100 cm (2-3 ft) tall specimens.

Light Grow this plant in bright filtered light during the active growth period and direct sunlight during the winter months.
Water Water plentifully and feed with a standard liquid fertilizer diluted to half-strength once a month during the active growth period. Water moderately in the winter.
Temperature The ideal temperature is around 18-24°C (65-75°F) but the parlour palm will tolerate a lower temperature of 12°C (55°F).
Humidity This plant needs high humidity. Stand the pot on a tray filled with moist pebbles.
Extra point The parlour palm will grow well in a pot that may appear to be much too small for it. Repot in spring but only when the plant has totally filled its pot with roots.

> ### Decorating tip
> *An ideal place to display the parlour palm is in the bathroom, perhaps on a low table or at the end of the bath. Here you can be sure there will be sufficient humidity for the plant to remain healthy.*

49

Chamaerops humilis

EUROPEAN FAN PALM

The European fan palm is a bushy plant that produces fan-shaped fronds on jagged stalks. Offsets grow around its base and the plant quickly forms thick clumps.

Light Grow in direct sunlight.
Water Water plentifully and feed with a standard liquid fertilizer once every two weeks from early spring to late autumn. Water sparingly during the winter rest period.
Temperature This plant is tolerant of a wide range of temperatures. It does best at 18-24°C (65-75°F), but will survive at 7°C (45°F).
Humidity This palm tolerates dry air and needs no extra humidity.

> ### Decorating tip
> *A mature palm, that has started to develop a short, brown hairy trunk, has a striking architectural quality and looks best standing on its own in a bright corner of a room.*

50

Chlorophytum comosum 'Vittatum'

SPIDER PLANT

When well-grown, a spider plant looks very decorative. Its delicately arching, striped leaves and yellow-stalked trailing stems, first carrying clusters of small white flowers, and later miniature replicas of the parent plant, provide year-round interest.

Light Grow the plant in bright filtered light from early spring to late autumn but move it into direct sunlight for the winter.

Water Water plentifully and feed with a standard liquid fertilizer once every two weeks during the active growth period. Water more moderately in the winter.

Temperature Normal room temperatures are suitable for a chlorophytum, with a winter minimum of 7°C (45°F).

Humidity This plant prefers increased humidity. Stand the pot on a tray of moist pebbles and mist-spray the foliage regularly.

Extra point A chlorophytum will develop thickened white root sections that push the potting mixture upwards as they develop. When repotting a plant, leave plenty of space between the pot rim and the surface of the mixture to allow for this.

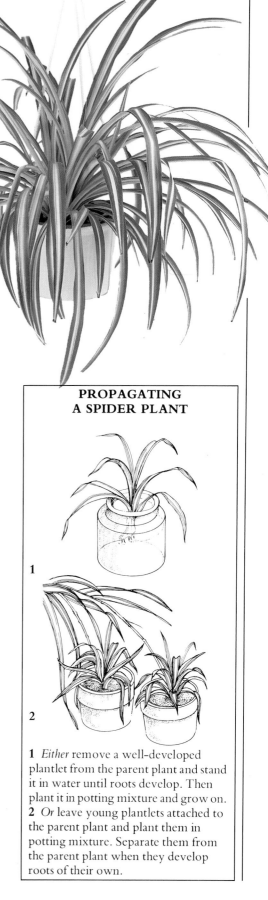

Decorating tip

Plant several rooted offsets in a large hanging basket and hang it in a well-lit window. With back-lighting the whole plant takes on a light yellowy-green hue. The trailing stems have lots of room to develop and will often produce "offspring" of their own, creating a cascading "waterfall" effect.

Training round a hoop *An unusual and attractive way to display a chlorophytum is to push a cane hoop into the potting mixture and then train the long trailing stems bearing plantlets around it. Secure the ends with plant ties.*

PROPAGATING A SPIDER PLANT

1 *Either* remove a well-developed plantlet from the parent plant and stand it in water until roots develop. Then plant it in potting mixture and grow on.
2 *Or* leave young plantlets attached to the parent plant and plant them in potting mixture. Separate them from the parent plant when they develop roots of their own.

51

Chrysalidocarpus lutescens
GOLDEN-FEATHER PALM

The striking feature of this palm is its slender, yellow leaf stalks and delicate appearance. The stems are clustered closely together at the base of the plant.

Light Grow the plant in bright filtered light from early spring to mid-autumn and in direct sunlight in winter.
Water Water plentifully and feed with a standard liquid fertilizer once every two weeks during the active growth period. Water moderately during the winter.
Temperature This palm enjoys warm room conditions and will not tolerate temperatures below 12°C (55°F).
Humidity This plant needs high humidity.

Decorating tip
Stand this elegant palm on the floor, at the side of a full-length window where its feathery appearance and rich golden colouring will be boldly displayed against the light.

52

Chrysanthemum morifolium hybrids
CHRYSANTHEMUM

The chrysanthemum is a temporary plant (see page 142) and should be discarded when its flowers die. Its double or single flowers appear in many colours.

Light Grow this plant in bright filtered light.
Water Soak the rootball periodically by standing the pot in a bowl filled with water. There is normally no need to feed this plant.
Temperature This plant prefers a cool temperature, ideally at around 12°C (55°F).
Humidity This plant prefers increased humidity.

Decorating tip
A chrysanthemum can be effectively displayed amongst a group of green foliage plants. The single or double flowers, in a whole range of colours, will provide decorative highlights.

53

Cineraria hybrids
(now officially *Senecio hybridus*)

CINERARIA

The cineraria produces large, striking flower-heads in strong or subtle colours, often with a white central "eye". This plant is a temporary flowering house plant (see page 142) and should be discarded when the flowers die.

Light Grow the plant in bright filtered light.
Water Soak the pot and rootball frequently in a bowl of water, to ensure that the potting mixture is kept permanently moist. Feed with a standard liquid fertilizer once every two weeks whilst flowering continues.
Temperature Grow the cineraria in a cool temperature to extend its flowering life.
Humidity High humidity is essential for this plant. Stand the pot on a tray of moist pebbles and regularly mist-spray the undersides of the large floppy leaves.

Decorating tip
Group several cinerarias together in a waterproof wicker basket and stand it on a low table where you can look down on to the mass of daisy-like flowers.

54

Cissus antarctica

KANGAROO VINE

This Australian climbing plant is a close relative of the grape vine. It has tooth-edged green leaves and clings to thin supports by means of forked tendrils. It grows very easily.

Light Grow the plant in bright filtered light throughout the year.
Water Water moderately and feed with a standard liquid fertilizer once every two weeks during the active growth period. Water sparingly during winter.
Temperature This plant will grow lustily in normal room temperatures, but a minimum temperature of 12°C (55°F) in winter is essential.
Humidity This plant will grow well in relatively dry air but prefers increased humidity if it is growing in a warm room. Stand the pot on a tray of moist pebbles.

Decorating tip
Train a cissus around a window frame on thin cord, allowing odd stems to stray and trail across the window to soften the sharp box-like lines.

55

Cissus rhombifolia

GRAPE IVY

This climbing plant grows quickly, clinging to supports with wiry tendrils.

Light Grow in bright filtered light.
Water Water moderately and feed with a standard liquid fertilizer every two weeks during the active growth period. Water sparingly in winter.
Temperature Normal room temperatures are suitable, with a minimum of 12°C (55°F) in winter.
Humidity This plant needs high humidity. Stand it on moist pebbles.

Decorating tip
Plant several small grape ivy plants in a large hanging basket and hang it near a sunny window for an attractive feature.

56

Citrofortunella mitis

CALAMONDIN ORANGE

This orange flowers and fruits regularly and always stays a manageable size.

Light Grow in direct sunlight.
Water Water moderately during the active growth period but more sparingly during the winter. Feed with a tomato-type liquid fertilizer (see page 133) once every two weeks while the plant is flowering.
Temperature Normal room temperatures are suitable.
Humidity This plant needs high humidity. Stand the pot on moist pebbles and mist-spray regularly.

Decorating tip
The citrofortunella can be in flower and in fruit at the same time, making a formal, ornamental decoration. Display it where the deliciously scented flowers can be most appreciated and the development of the small fruits closely observed.

57

Cleistocactus strausii

SILVER TORCH

This slender cactus is densely covered with silvery white spines. The stem often branches at the base, and the plant can grow to 120 cm (4 ft) high.

Light Grow in direct sunlight.
Water Water moderately and feed with a standard liquid fertilizer once every two weeks during the active growth period. Water sparingly during the winter.
Temperature Normal room temperatures are suitable from spring to autumn but a winter temperature of 7-12°C (45-55°F) is preferred.
Humidity This plant enjoys dry air.
Extra point A small silver torch needs to be potted on each spring, but an older plant needs attention only every second or third year.

Decorating tip
Show off this slim silvery plant by growing it among fleshy-leaved plants such as Crassula ovata and smooth-leaved echeverias, like Echeveria derenbergii, in a small dish garden.

58

Clivia miniata

KAFIR LILY

The strap-shaped leathery leaves of the clivia grow in two ranks from a thickened base, much like a leek. Very early in spring a pale flower-head can be seen tucked inside the crease of the leaves, slightly off-centre, and this grows slowly on a stout stem. At its top appear twenty or so bright orange, trumpet-shaped flowers. Occasionally yellow or apricot-coloured varieties can be found.

Light Grow this plant in bright filtered light. Insufficient light results in no flowers being produced. A window-sill that receives early morning or late afternoon sun is best. A plant can stand out of doors during the summer months in a sheltered and partially shaded position, but it must gradually be accustomed to the brighter light or its leaves will become "scorched".

Water Water plentifully, ensuring that the potting mixture is kept thoroughly moist, once the flower-head is well clear of the crease of leaves and continue until late autumn. Feed with a standard liquid fertilizer once every two weeks for the same period. Stop watering and feeding at the end of autumn and keep the potting mixture completely dry until early in spring when the flower-head begins to grow. Then gradually water normally again.

Temperature Normal room temperatures are suitable during the active growth period. In late autumn move the clivia to a cooler position, ideally at around 10°C (50°F) for its winter rest period. This rest is essential if a plant is to flower the following spring.

Humidity The clivia is tolerant of dry air and does not require extra humidity.

Extra point The clivia develops many thick roots that begin to appear on the surface of the potting mixture as the plant grows. Clivias flower best when their roots are confined and they should only be repotted when this is essential. When the plant is repotted remove the offsets and pot them up separately in soil-based potting mixture.

Decorating tip
The clivia is a very bold-looking plant and is best displayed on its own. It needs plenty of space to develop fully, as a mature plant in a large pot can produce two or more flower-heads, so it is best not to clutter ornaments and other plants around it.

PROPAGATING A CLIVIA

1 A clivia can be propagated when it has developed offsets and the roots are visible.

2 Remove the plant from its pot and examine it to find where each offset is attached.

3 Carefully cut off an offset that has healthy roots and at least three leaves.

4 Plant the separated offset in rooting mixture. Take care not to damage the roots.

59

Codiaeum variegatum pictum

CROTON

The size, shape and colour of this plant's leaves vary enormously. They may be long and narrow, almost oval or twisted into a spiral, and coloured green, red, orange or bright yellow.

Light Grow in bright filtered light for most of the year but move to a sunny window in winter.
Water Water plentifully and feed with a standard liquid fertilizer once every two weeks during the active growth period. Water moderately during the winter.
Temperature Normal room temperatures are suitable, with a minimum of 12°C (55°F).
Humidity This plant prefers extra humidity; mist-spray it in warm weather to discourage red spider mites.

Decorating tip
The croton can grow into a bushy shrub 1 m (3 ft) tall, and as such is best displayed as a solitary feature to brighten up a room. To complement the warm colouring of its leaves, use a red or orange container.

60

Coleus blumei hybrids

FLAME NETTLE

The flame nettle is usually grown as a temporary house plant (see page 142) and thrown away at the beginning of winter, but a specially prized plant can be kept (or a cutting taken) and over-wintered with difficulty.

Light Grow in bright filtered light from spring to autumn and direct sunlight in winter.
Water Water plentifully at all times. Feed with a standard liquid fertilizer once every two weeks during the active growth period.
Temperature Normal room temperatures suit this plant, with a minimum of 12°C (55°F) in winter.
Humidity High humidity is essential for this plant. Stand the pot on a tray of moist pebbles.

Decorating tip
The coleus is one of the most striking and colourful house plants, with its many varied colours and leaf patterns. Group several plants together in a simple decorative bowl and stand it in a bright window.

61

Columnea gloriosa

GOLDFISH PLANT

The fiery-red, hooded flowers of this plant contrast beautifully with the purplish hairs that cover the leaves. Its stems can reach 1 m (3 ft) long.

Light Grow the plant in bright filtered light for most of the growing period but move it to a sunny window for the winter months.
Water Water the goldfish plant sparingly throughout the year. Feed with a tomato-type liquid fertilizer (see page 133) once every month during the active growth period.
Temperature Normal room temperatures are suitable, an ideal being 18-24°C (65-75°F).
Humidity This plant needs a very high level of humidity. Stand the pot on a tray of moist pebbles and mist-spray it frequently.

Decorating tip
The beauty of this plant is only fully appreciated when it is grown in a hanging basket. Hang it in a brightly lit window, where the purplish-brown trails of leaves prove a perfect foil for the red flowers.

62

Cordyline terminalis

TI PLANT

The large, shiny leaves of this plant can be several different colours, ranging from deep red to soft pink.

Light Grow in bright filtered light throughout the year.
Water Water plentifully and feed with a standard liquid fertilizer once every two weeks during the active growth period. Water sparingly during the winter.
Temperature Grow in temperatures between 18-24°C (65-75°F) from early spring until mid-autumn. A cordyline needs a rest period in winter at about 15°C (60°F).
Humidity This plant needs high humidity. Stand the pot on a large tray of moist pebbles and mist-spray the plant on very hot days. The thin leaves are liable to be marked and spoiled by a low humidity level.

Decorating tip
Group several cordylines with strong red leaf colouring together in a warm-coloured room to make a sumptuous display.

63

Cotyledon undulata

SILVER CROWN

This succulent can grow up to 50 cm (20 in) tall. Orange coloured flowers grow on mature plants.

Light Grow in direct sunlight.
Water Water moderately and feed with a standard liquid fertilizer once every two weeks during the active growth period. Water sparingly during the winter.
Temperature This plant is able to withstand high temperatures whilst light levels are high. In the winter, however, it should be kept cool.
Humidity This plant tolerates dry air and does not need any extra humidity to be provided.
Extra point Be careful not to handle the leaves more than necessary, as the thin, silvery "bloom" or meal that covers them is spoiled if touched.

Decorating tip
Display the plant on a low table in a brightly-lit window during the day, and move it under a table lamp at night so you can enjoy the silvery scalloped leaf edges.

64

Crassula falcata

SICKLE PLANT

This plant is striking both for its greyish-green, sickle-shaped leaves and its many small but brilliant scarlet flowers that grow from the large flattened flower-head.

Light Grow in direct sunlight throughout the year.
Water Water moderately and feed with a standard liquid fertilizer once every two weeks during the active growth period. Water very sparingly during the winter.
Temperature Normal room temperatures are suitable for most of the year, but a cool winter rest at around 10°C (50°F) is recommended.
Humidity This plant is unaffected by dry air and needs no extra humidity.

Decorating tip
Display this relatively small succulent in a cactus garden amongst other slow growing and decorative cacti and succulents.

65

Crassula lycopodioides

WATCH-CHAIN CRASSULA

This small, shrubby crassula rarely grows taller than 30 cm (1 ft) high. Its stems are completely covered with minute leaves that are packed tightly together in four rows. The greenish-coloured flowers are also very tiny, appearing in spring and summer.

Light Grow in direct sunlight throughout the year.
Water Water moderately and feed with a standard liquid fertilizer once every two weeks during the active growth period. Water sparingly during the winter.
Temperature Tolerant of a wide range of temperatures, this crassula needs a minimum winter temperature of 10°C (50°F).
Humidity This plant is unaffected by dry air and needs no extra humidity.

Decorating tip
With its unusual shape, this crassula can be used to add interest and height to an arrangement of small succulent plants.

66

Crassula ovata

JADE PLANT

This plant's common name comes from its shiny jade-green leaves. There are a number of varieties, one of the best being *C.o.* 'Hummel's Sunset', which has yellow, gold and red liberally splashed on its leaves.

Light Grow in direct sunlight.
Water Water moderately and feed with a standard liquid fertilizer once every two weeks from early spring to mid-autumn. Water sparingly in the winter rest period.
Temperature This plant is tolerant of a range of temperatures during the active growth period, but requires a winter rest at around 10°C (50°F).
Humidity This plant is unaffected by dry air and needs no extra humidity.

Decorating tip
A well-grown crassula can look extremely decorative with its glossy green leaves. Grow a pair of crassulas to about 60 cm (2 ft) tall and stand one on either side of a full-length window.

67

Cryptanthus bivittatus

EARTH STAR

This plant is called earth star because of its low-growing habit and star shape. It can spread to as much as 30 cm (1 ft) wide; its height rarely exceeds 2.5 cm (1 in).

Light Grow in direct sunlight for the strongest leaf colour.
Water Water sparingly at all times. Like all bromeliads (see page 34), the cryptanthus can take moisture from the air. Feed with a standard liquid fertilizer two or three times during the active growth period.
Temperature This plant grows well in normal room temperatures.
Humidity High humidity is essential. Stand the pot on moist pebbles and mist-spray frequently, particularly on warm days.
Extra points Small clusters of white flowers grow from near the centre of the rosette of leaves of a mature plant. After a rosette has flowered once it then dies. Offsets appear between the leaves for propagation.

Decorating tip
This rather unassuming plant relies on its shape and subtle colouring for appeal. Grow it in a shallow pan or small glass container on a table or desk, so you can look down on the intricate leaf patterning.

68

Cryptanthus bromelioides 'Tricolor'

RAINBOW STAR

The rainbow star is much looser in appearance than other cryptanthuses and very colourful. In bright light the paler sections of the leaves are suffused with a lovely carmine red.

Light Grow in bright filtered light from early spring to autumn but move to direct sunlight for the winter.
Water Water moderately at all times. Feed with a standard liquid fertilizer two or three times during the active growth period.
Temperature Normal room temperatures are suitable, with a minimum of 12°C (55°F) during the winter rest period.
Humidity Provide high humidity by regular mist-spraying and standing the pot on a tray of moist pebbles.

Decorating tip
Display this very colourful plant in a well-lit window during the daytime and move it under a table lamp for the evening. It will enjoy the extra light and look stunning.

69

Cyanotis kewensis

TEDDY-BEAR PLANT

The trailing stems of this tradescantia relative may reach 30 cm (1 ft) in length. They are covered in rusty-brown hairs, which give the plant its common name.

Light Grow in bright filtered light from early spring to late autumn but move to direct sunlight for the winter.
Water Water moderately throughout the year. Feed with a standard liquid fertilizer once every two months during the active growth period.
Temperature Normal room temperatures are suitable.
Humidity This plant needs high humidity. Stand the pot on a large tray filled with moist pebbles, and mist-spray the plant regularly.

Decorating tip
Plant a cyanotis in a small hanging basket and display it in a brightly-lit bathroom or kitchen window, where the air is likely to be humid for most of the day.

70

Cycas revoluta

SAGO PALM

The leaves of the cycas are arranged in a formal rosette shape. They are tough and needle-like and grow from a rounded, woody base. This plant grows *very* slowly.

Light Grow in direct sunlight throughout the year.
Water Water moderately and feed with a standard liquid fertilizer once every two weeks during the active growth period. Water very sparingly in winter, giving only enough to prevent the potting mixture from drying out completely.
Temperature This plant is tolerant of a wide range of temperatures, but needs a temperature of at least 12°C (55°F) in winter.
Humidity The cycas is unaffected by dry air and needs no extra humidity.

Decorating tip
Large cycases are greatly prized (and very expensive) because of their striking appearance and hard-wearing leaves. They look best displayed on their own, as specimen plants, so their formal rosette shape can be appreciated.

71

Cyclamen persicum hybrids

CYCLAMEN

The cyclamen is best treated as a temporary plant (see page 142) and thrown away when its flowers die, although with a lot of care it can sometimes be kept for another year. It is a tuberous-rooted plant (see page 142) and can be bought in bloom from early autumn through to spring. The flowers may be white, red, pink or purple.

Light Give this plant bright filtered light, but keep it out of direct sunlight, which might scorch the leaves.

Water During the active growth period water the cyclamen by standing the pot in a deep dish of water for half an hour. This avoids wetting the tuber, which can rot. Repeat when the surface of the mixture feels dry. Feed with a standard liquid fertilizer every two weeks.

Temperature Keep the plant cool at all times, so that its flowers last longer: warmth will shorten the plant's life. A temperature of about 12°C (55°F) is ideal.

Humidity This plant prefers increased humidity. Stand it on a large saucer filled with moist pebbles.

Decorating tip
With their distinctive flowers, cyclamens look most attractive growing in a large group. Collect three or four cyclamen plants together, either all of the same colour or a mixture of strong pinks and white-flowered kinds. Then arrange them in a wicker basket or group them on a table top for a very pleasing and colourful winter decoration.

Watering a cyclamen
Stand the cyclamen in a dish of water for half an hour. Then drain away any remaining water.

Extra point To keep a cyclamen for a second year, stop watering and feeding it when the foliage yellows and dries in early summer, and rest the tuber in its pot. Lay the pot on its side outdoors during the summer months, and when new leaves appear in midsummer, repot the plant into fresh potting mixture, bring it indoors into bright filtered light and treat as before to allow it to grow on.

72

Cyperus alternifolius

UMBRELLA PLANT

Cyperus alternifolius is a bog plant (see page 142) with unusual reed-like stems that are topped with "leaves" arranged like the spokes of an umbrella. This plant likes its roots to be in constantly wet conditions.

Light This plant needs bright filtered light during the active growth period and ideally direct sunlight during the winter months.
Water Stand the pot in a deep saucer kept full of water so that the mixture can take up its water needs. Feed with a standard liquid fertilizer once every two weeks during the active growth period. Occasionally give the plant a thorough watering from above to flush out any salts that may have built up in the potting mixture.
Temperature Normal room temperatures are suitable for a cyperus, with a winter minimum of 10°C (50°F).
Humidity This plant needs high humidity. The water-filled saucer and moist potting mixture ensure this.
Extra point Handle the plant very carefully as bent or damaged stems will not recover.

Decorating tip
This plant looks effective displayed near a window where its grassy stems can be silhouetted against the light.

73

Cyrtomium falcatum

HOLLY FERN

This decorative plant has leathery frond sections that resemble holly leaves in outline. It is easy to manage, tolerant of a certain amount of neglect and is long lasting.

Light Although able to survive short periods of poor light, the holly fern does best in bright filtered light.
Water Water moderately throughout the year. Feed with a standard liquid fertilizer once every two weeks during the active growth period.
Temperature Normal room temperatures are suitable with a winter minimum of 10°C (50°F).
Humidity This plant prefers increased humidity if being grown in a warm room. Stand the pot on a tray filled with moist pebbles.

Decorating tip
Use a holly fern to brighten up a draughty porch or unheated conservatory where few other house plants will grow.

74

Davallia canariensis

DEERSFOOT FERN

This fern gets its common name from the pale brown fur that grows on its creeping rhizomes.

Light Grow the plant in medium light throughout the year.
Water Water moderately at all times. Feed with a standard liquid fertilizer once a month during the active growth period.
Temperature The davallia grows well in a wide range of temperatures, but there might be some leaf loss if the temperature falls below 12°C (55°F).
Humidity This plant prefers increased humidity when the temperature rises. Stand it on a tray of moist pebbles.

Decorating tip
The davallia is an ideal plant to grow in a hanging basket. Its creeping rhizomes, which are interesting features in their own right, will grow over the edge of the container, allowing the fronds to trail.

75

Dieffenbachia maculata

DUMB-CANE

This plant is also called spotted dumb-cane, because of the many cream coloured spots on its large leaves. It is poisonous, so wash your hands after handling it, and stand it where young children cannot reach it.

Light Grow in bright filtered light, from early spring to autumn, and in direct sunlight during winter.
Water Water moderately all year. Feed with a standard liquid fertilizer once every two weeks during the active growth period.

Temperature The dumb-cane likes warm temperatures with a minimum of 15°C (60°F).
Humidity This plant needs high humidity. Stand it on moist pebbles and mist-spray frequently.

Decorating tip
The large, strongly variegated leaves of this plant make it very striking. Arrange two or three plants together in one large container and display it on a low table or on the floor in a large bathroom.

76

Dizygotheca elegantissima

FALSE ARALIA

The false aralia has a light, open look and unusual coppery-red colouring.

Light Grow in bright filtered light, avoiding the hot sun.
Water Water sparingly at all times. Feed with a standard liquid fertilizer once every two weeks during the active growth period.
Temperature The false aralia likes warm temperatures, with a minimum of 15°C (60°F).
Humidity A high level of humidity is essential. Stand the pot on a tray of moist pebbles and mist-spray the plant frequently. The spraying will also discourage red spider mites which are liable to attack this plant.

Decorating tip
Grow a false aralia in a mixed group of bold-leaved plants, such as Aglaonema crispum *and* Codiaeum variegatum pictum, *where its delicate foliage will provide contrast and lighten the display.*

77

Dracaena deremensis 'Warneckii'

This dracaena has several white stripes running the length of its sword-shaped, arching leaves, which are arranged in a loose rosette shape around a woody stem. A plant can grow to 120-180 cm (4-6 ft) tall, retaining most of its leaves if well looked after, but losing the lower ones if it suffers some neglect. There are some new varieties of *D. deremensis* that offer unique colouring amongst house plants: *D.d.* 'Yellow Edge' with strong yellow striping, and *D.d.* 'Lemon and Lime' with brilliant lime green striping.

Light Grow the plant in bright filtered light from early spring to late autumn, and in direct sunlight during the winter months.
Water Water plentifully and feed with a standard liquid fertilizer once every two weeks during the active growth period. Water moderately during the winter.
Temperature This plant enjoys very warm temperatures, at around 18-24°C (65-75°F) during the active growth period, with just a drop of about 6°C (10°F) during winter. In a prolonged period of low temperatures the leaves of the dracaena first droop and then eventually drop off.
Humidity The secret of success in looking after this plant is high humidity. Stand the pot on a large tray filled with moist pebbles and mist-spray frequently.

Decorating tip
Display a dracaena on its own in a modern setting, where its gracefully arching leaves with their bold striping will be clearly seen.

78

Dracaena fragrans 'Massangeana'

CORN PLANT

The corn plant's arching leaves have a wide central band of yellowy-green. The plant can grow 180 cm (6 ft) tall.

Light Grow the plant in bright filtered light.
Water Water plentifully and feed with a standard liquid fertilizer once every two weeks from early spring to late autumn. Water moderately during winter.
Temperature Provide a temperature of about 18-24°C (65-75°F) with a minimum of 15°C (60°F) in winter.
Humidity High humidity is essential for this plant.

Decorating tip
Stand this bold-looking plant on its own on a staircase landing or where there is some height (and enough light) so the plant can be allowed to develop to its full potential.

79

Dracaena marginata

MADAGASCAR DRAGON TREE

Capable of growing to 180 cm (6 ft) tall, this dracaena can be bought as a single rosette of thin leaves, or as a tall, bare stem bearing several rosettes of leaves at the top of branching stems.

Light Grow the plant in bright filtered light.
Water Water plentifully and feed with a standard liquid fertilizer once every two weeks during the active growth period. Water moderately during winter.

Temperature Normal room temperatures are suitable.
Humidity This plant needs high humidity to thrive.
Extra point As the plant grows older, the lower leaves will turn yellow. This is nothing to be alarmed about, and when it occurs, simply pull them gently off the stem.

Decorating tip
For an attractive arrangement, group several dracaenas of varying heights together. Their graceful arching shapes will create a strong silhouette.

80

Dracaena reflexa variegata

SONG OF INDIA

This plant was called *Pleomele* for many years. It is only grown in the home in the variegated form, being prized for its strong yellow and lime-green striped leaves.

Light Grow in bright filtered light, avoiding direct summer sun.
Water Water moderately and feed with a standard liquid fertilizer once every two weeks during the active growth period. Water sparingly in the winter months.
Temperature Grow this plant in a warm room, with a minimum of 15°C (60°F) in winter.
Humidity This plant thrives in high humidity. Stand the pot on a tray of moist pebbles and mist-spray the plant regularly.

81

Echeveria derenbergii

PAINTED LADY

This plant produces orange flowers in spring and early summer.

Light Grow in direct sunlight.
Water Water sparingly, and avoid wetting the fleshy leaves, as water lodging in them can cause rot. Feed with a standard liquid fertilizer once every two weeks during the active growth period.
Temperature This plant will tolerate normal room temperatures for most of the year, but in winter it prefers a cool temperature of about 10-12°C (50-55°F).
Humidity The echeveria prefers dry air and needs no extra humidity.
Extra point Take care when handling this plant, as the waxy, silvery "bloom" that covers the leaves can easily be rubbed off.

82

Echeveria harmsii

The stems of this unusual echeveria can grow up to 30 cm (1 ft) tall. Its red flowers appear on long stalks in late spring and early summer.

Light Grow in direct sunlight throughout the year.
Water Water moderately and feed with a standard liquid fertilizer once every two weeks from early spring to mid-autumn. Gradually decrease watering, and then water very sparingly in winter.
Temperature Normal room temperatures are suitable for most of the year, but the plant needs a cool winter rest at around 12°C (55°F).
Humidity This plant is tolerant of dry air and does not need extra humidity to be provided.

Echinocactus grusonii

GOLDEN BARREL

This plant is ball-shaped with distinct ribs along its sides. Strong yellow spines grow along the ribs.

Light Grow in direct sunlight. The golden barrel can stand outside in the summer in a sheltered position in full sun. This will enrich and intensify the colour of the spines.
Water Water moderately and feed with a tomato-type liquid fertilizer (see page 133) once a month during the active growth period. Water very sparingly during winter.
Temperature Normal room temperatures are suitable for the growing season but a cool winter rest at around 10°C (50°F) is important.
Humidity This Mexican desert plant is able to withstand dry air.

Decorating tip

A medium- to large-sized plant makes a distinctive, strong shape that should be displayed on its own, ideally on a sunny window-sill.

Epiphyllum hybrids

ORCHID CACTUS

The striking flowers of this cactus may be white, red or orange.

Light Grow in bright filtered light.
Water Water plentifully and feed with a tomato-type liquid fertilizer (see page 133) every two weeks during spring and summer. Water sparingly in the winter months.
Temperature This plant prefers warmth, with a winter rest period at around 12°C (55°F).
Humidity High humidity is essential for the epiphyllum. Stand it on a tray filled with moist pebbles.

Decorating tip

Train the fleshy stems up thin canes for a glorious array of blooms.

85

Epipremnum aureum

DEVIL'S IVY

This plant was called *Scindapsus aureus* for many years. Its heart-shaped leaves vary in size and variegation. Climbing or trailing stems can grow to 2 m (6 ft) long.

Light Grow the plant in bright filtered light from early spring to late autumn, and in direct sunlight in winter.
Water Water moderately and feed with a standard liquid fertilizer once every two weeks during the active growth period. Water sparingly during winter.
Temperature Normal room temperatures are suitable, with a winter rest at around 15°C (60°F).
Humidity High humidity is essential for this plant to thrive. Stand the pot on a tray of moist pebbles.

Decorating tip

Make a bold feature of this plant by training it up a moist moss-covered pole until a dense column of foliage is produced.

86

Euphorbia milii

CROWN OF THORNS

The crown of thorns can produce its small flowers and more colourful bracts all the year. Several varieties are available with cream, salmon-pink or bright red bracts.

Light Grow this plant in direct sunlight.
Water Water moderately and feed with a standard liquid fertilizer once every two weeks during the active growth period. Water sparingly during winter.
Temperature Provide a minimum of 12°C (55°F).
Humidity This plant grows well in dry air.
Extra point The cut stems exude a milky white latex that can cause irritation to the skin.

Decorating tip

Display a mature euphorbia on a corner shelf or other surface at eye level, where its rather gaunt, spiny stems will provide an interesting sculptural feature.

87

Euphorbia pulcherrima

POINSETTIA

Traditionally the poinsettia only produced flower-heads after a period of days with few daylight hours, but many modern varieties now bloom from mid-autumn until well into the spring. Creamy white, pale pink and cream-streaked pink varieties are available as well as the more common red "flowered" kinds. Low growing poinsettias are also popular as house plants. The actual flowers are insignificant, the showy part of the plant being the bracts (see page 142), that can remain decorative for two months. Most poinsettias are treated as temporary plants (see page 142), displayed in the home for a short time and thrown away when past their best, although with specialist knowledge, it is possible to keep a plant for a second year.

Light Grow a poinsettia in bright filtered light at all times.

Water Water sparingly, waiting until there is a *little* drooping of the leaves before giving more. Over-watering quickly results in leaf fall. No feeding is necessary.
Temperature The bracts will last for longer in a cool temperature ideally at around 15-18°C (60-65°F).
Humidity This plant tolerates dry air and needs no extra humidity.
Extra point The sap of this plant, which is a milky white colour, is poisonous, so wash your hands after handling the plant and keep it out of reach of young children.

> **Decorating tip**
> *With their colourful bracts blooming over Christmas, poinsettias make an obvious tabletop decoration. Group several cardinal-red coloured plants together for a traditional festive air.*

88

Exacum affine

GERMAN VIOLET

Treated as a temporary house plant (see page 142), the German violet will remain in bloom for six to eight weeks. Lavender coloured flowers are the most common, but deeper blue and white-flowered kinds are also occasionally available.

Light Grow this plant in bright filtered light.
Water The German violet is usually bought in a relatively small pot and the potting mixture dries out surprisingly quickly. Water plentifully, and feed with a standard liquid fertilizer once every two weeks to encourage further blooming.
Temperature Normal room temperatures are suitable.
Humidity This plant prefers extra humidity. Stand the pot on a tray of moist pebbles.

> **Decorating tip**
> *Group several of these inexpensive plants together in a shallow container and display this on a brightly lit window-sill. Move the basket under a table lamp for the evening where the plants will appreciate the extra light and you can enjoy the plants for a longer period.*

89

Fatshedera lizei

TREE IVY

This plant displays attributes from both of its parents – fatsia and hedera (ivy). Its stems are most like those of ivy, while its leaves are fatsia-like but scaled down in size.

Light This plant grows best in bright filtered light.
Water Water moderately and feed with a standard liquid fertilizer once every two weeks during the active growth period. Water sparingly during winter.

Temperature This plant will grow well in a wide range of temperatures.
Humidity In a warm room the fatshedera prefers to have increased humidity. Stand it on a tray of moist pebbles and mist-spray the plant frequently to discourage red spider mites that are liable to attack.
Extra point The stems are often too weak to support the plant, so thin canes should be used to keep the plant from sprawling.

Decorating tip
Create an attractive green column of foliage by growing several plants in the same pot and training them up thin canes.

90

Fatsia japonica

JAPANESE ARALIA

The Japanese aralia can grow up to 90-120 cm (3-4 ft) tall indoors. Its shiny, fingered leaves can grow up to 37 cm (15 in) across.

Light Grow in bright filtered light throughout the year.
Water Water plentifully and feed with a standard liquid fertilizer once every two weeks during the active growth period. Water moderately during the winter.
Temperature This plant will thrive in a wide range of temperatures.
Humidity This plant prefers increased humidity. Stand the pot on a tray of moist pebbles and mist-spray the foliage frequently.
Extra point Fatsias can be bought in all sizes, from small seedlings to tall, impressive shrubs. Any plant that grows too big can be cut back to the required size in spring.

Decorating tip
This fatsia has a bold, architectural appearance. Stand a mature plant on its own beside a full-length window, so its bushy outline and large, glossy leaves can be appreciated.

FERNS

Ferns do not produce flowers, or seeds, but instead they reproduce by means of spores which appear on the undersides of the leaves. The leaves are called fronds and can be simple in outline, but are more often made up in an intricate way of many thin, small segments.

Some ferns are *terrestrial,* which means they grow on the ground; others are *epiphytic,* growing on the branches of trees and taking their moisture and food from the humus in bark crevices. Most ferns have a rhizomatous base that creeps along the soil or over moss and forest debris on the trees. This rhizome stores food and water.

Cultivation
In general, ferns dislike hot summer sunlight, preferring some shade. High humidity is also essential. Ferns need to be watered plentifully. A well-drained potting mixture is essential, but make sure it never dries out.

163
Pteris cretica
Cretan brake

32
Blechnum gibbum

21
Asplenium nidus
Bird's nest fern

140
Pellaea rotundifolia
Button fern

73
Cyrtomium falcatum
Holly fern

74
Davallia canariensis
Deersfoot fern

159
Polypodium aureum
Hare's foot fern

126
Nephrolepis exaltata
Sword fern

2
Adiantum raddianum
Delta maidenhair

20
Asplenium bulbiferum
Hen-and-chicken fern

155
Platycerium bifurcatum
Staghorn fern

91

Ficus benjamina

WEEPING FIG

This plant gets its common name from the way its leaves "hang" on short leaf stalks on drooping branch-ends. There are plants ranging from 20 cm (8 in) to 180 cm (6 ft) tall.

Light Grow the plant in bright filtered light for most of the year, but move it to a sunny position for the winter months.

Water Water moderately and feed with a standard liquid fertilizer once every two weeks during the active growth period. Water sparingly during the winter.
Temperature The weeping fig will thrive in normal room temperatures, with a winter minimum temperature of 15°C (60°F).

Humidity This plant prefers increased humidity in a warm room. Stand the pot on a tray of moist pebbles and mist-spray the plant frequently. Regular spraying helps to discourage red spider mites from attacking.
Extra point The weeping fig will grow well in a pot that may appear to be too small for it. Repot only when it is essential.

Decorating tip
This ficus is a very graceful, ornamental plant that will add a touch of elegance to any living room, whether modern or period. Stand it on the floor near to a full-length window.

92

Ficus elastica 'Decora'

RUBBER PLANT

The rubber plant is very easy to grow indoors. It has perky, dark green, glossy leaves that grow almost horizontally from the stem.

Light This plant prefers bright filtered light.
Water Water moderately and feed with a standard liquid fertilizer once every two weeks during the active growth period. Water sparingly during the winter.
Temperature The rubber plant grows well in a wide range of temperatures but needs at least 12°C (55°F) during the winter.
Humidity This plant prefers increased humidity in a warm room. Stand it on a tray of moist pebbles.

Decorating tip
Although the rubber plant can look impressive growing in splendid isolation, a group of three plants together can look very striking indeed.

93

Ficus lyrata
FIDDLE-LEAF FIG

The large violin-shaped leaves of this plant have a crinkled surface. The fig can grow to 120 cm (4 ft) tall.

Light Grow in bright filtered light throughout the year.
Water Water moderately and feed with a standard liquid fertilizer once every two weeks from spring through to autumn. Water sparingly during the winter months.
Temperature Normal room temperatures are suitable.
Humidity High humidity is essential. Stand the plant on moist pebbles and mist-spray regularly.

Decorating tip
This plant is best displayed in a large, open space, such as a landing or hallway, where it can become a dramatic focal point.

94

Ficus pumila
CREEPING FIG

The creeping fig has thin, crinkly, heart-shaped leaves and a creeping or trailing habit. Stems can reach several metres long or the plant can be kept compact and bushy by frequent nipping out of the growing tips.

Light Grow the creeping fig in medium light.
Water Water moderately throughout the year but never allow the potting mixture to become dry or the thin leaves will shrivel and not recover. Feed with a standard liquid fertilizer once every two weeks during the active growth period.
Temperature This plant is tolerant of a wide range of temperatures, with a minimum of 10°C (50°F).
Humidity The creeping fig needs a high level of humidity. Stand the pot on a tray of moist pebbles and mist-spray the plant regularly.

Decorating tip
Train a creeping fig up a moss-covered pole to make a dense column of green. The moss must be sprayed regularly to keep it moist, so as to encourage the plant's aerial roots to grow into it.

95

Ficus retusa 'Green Gem'
LAUREL FIG

This plant has the same shape as *Ficus benjamina* (see page 64) but its leaves are blunter and more rounded.

Light Grow in bright filtered light.
Water Water moderately and feed with a standard liquid fertilizer once every two weeks during the active growth period. Water sparingly during the winter.
Temperature Normal room temperatures are suitable.
Humidity The laurel fig prefers extra humidity in a warm room; stand the plant on moist pebbles.

Decorating tip
This plant is very amenable to training into various shapes. Nip out the growing tips to train the plant into an unusual globe, pyramid, or columnar shape, and display it on a low table top.

96

Fittonia verschaffeltii
SNAKESKIN PLANT

The fittonia is a low-growing, creeping plant with small, beautifully marked leaves. As it grows it forms a neat mound or hummock of foliage. There is also a silver-veined form, *F.v. argyroneura,* and a dwarf variety of that plant called 'Nana'. Fittonia flowers are insignificant and are best nipped out as soon as they appear.

Light The fittonia is a tropical rain-forest plant that only needs medium light, not direct sunlight, during the active growth period. During the winter, keep the plant in a brighter position to retain the strong leaf colouring and contrast.
Water Water moderately through-out the year. The leaves shrivel and are spoiled if the plant dries out, while the stems can rot if the potting mixture becomes too wet. Feed with a standard liquid fertilizer once every two weeks during the active growth period.
Temperature This plant enjoys warmth and prefers temperatures of between 21-24°C (70-75°F). Avoid keeping the plant in fluctuating temperatures and draughts.

Humidity A high level of humidity is important. Stand the pot on a saucer or tray of moist pebbles and mist-spray the plant on warm days.

Decorating tip
Fittonias are excellent plants for growing in a terrarium or bottle garden, as they have shallow roots and thrive in humid air. Stand the terrarium or bottle garden on a low surface where you can look down on the lovely network of leaves.

97

Grevillea robusta
SILK-OAK

The silk-oak is a fast-growing evergreen shrub with finely divided, fern-like foliage. It can be bought as a very small plant or as a 1 m (3-4 ft) tall mature specimen, and is often found in trays of mixed ferns.

Light This plant enjoys the sun, and will grow well in direct sunlight or bright filtered light.
Water Water moderately and feed with a standard liquid fertilizer once every two weeks during the active growth period. Water sparingly during winter.
Temperature This plant is tolerant of a wide range of temperatures, but should have a minimum of 10°C (50°F) in winter.
Humidity The silk-oak prefers increased humidity if it is growing in a warm room. Stand the pot on a tray of moist pebbles.

Decorating tip
Plant a young grevillea with a mixture of other plants, such as peperomia and maranta, in a trough or bowl, where their finely cut leaves can provide interesting contrast.

98

Guzmania lingulata

SCARLET STAR

The leaves of this bromeliad can be up to 45 cm (1½ ft) long and up to 3 cm (1¼ in) wide. They are soft and shiny with smooth edges. The central flower spike remains decorative for some months, although the actual flowers are short-lived.

Light This plant needs bright filtered light throughout the year. If there is insufficient light, the plant will not produce flowers.
Water Water plentifully, keeping the potting mixture moist at all times. The central rosette of leaves will hold some water, and this should be topped up regularly. Unpolluted rainwater is best, as this does not mark the leaves. Feed with a standard liquid fertilizer once every two weeks during the active growth period.
Temperature Normal room temperatures are suitable, with a minimum of 15°C (60°F).
Humidity This plant needs high humidity. Stand the pot on a tray filled with moist pebbles and mist-spray the plant frequently.

Watering a guzmania *Keep the central rosette of leaves topped up with water.*

Decorating tip
The brightly-coloured flower spike is the most attractive part of the plant and is particularly long-lasting. Plant several guzmanias together to make a cheerful splash of colour in a room.

99

Gynura aurantiaca

PURPLE VELVET PLANT

This rather sprawling plant is grown for its purple velvety leaves. It produces insignificant flowers of a strong orange colour, but these have an unpleasant smell and are best nipped out when they appear.

Light Grow in direct sunlight, as only then will the leaves take on their strong colouring.
Water Water moderately but allow some drying out of the potting mixture between applications. Avoid wetting the hairy leaves. Feed with a standard liquid fertilizer once every two weeks during the active growth period.
Temperature The gynura grows well in normal room temperatures, with a minimum of 12°C (55°F).
Humidity This plant prefers increased humidity if it is grown in a warm room. Stand it on a tray filled with moist pebbles.

Decorating tip
This plant can look wonderful when grown in a hanging basket in a sunny window, where the light will enhance the strong purple colouring of the leaves.

100

Haworthia margaritifera

PEARL PLANT

This low-growing, succulent plant has fleshy, dark green leaves, liberally spotted with small, white bumps. In midsummer, a long flower stalk is produced, carrying greenish-white tubular flowers.

Light Grow this plant in bright filtered light.
Water Water moderately throughout the active growth period, and sparingly in winter. A plant grown in a soil-based potting mixture does not need feeding.

Temperature Normal room temperatures are suitable for most of the year, but provide a winter rest period at around 10°C (50°F).
Humidity This plant needs high humidity to thrive. Stand the pot on a tray of moist pebbles.

> **Decorating tip**
> *Display the pearl plant in a small dish or cactus garden and stand this where it can be seen in close-up, such as on a desk top or sunny shelf.*

101

Hedera canariensis

CANARY IVY

The leaves of this ivy can grow to 13-16 cm (5-6 in) wide.

Light Grow in bright filtered light.
Water Water moderately and feed once every two weeks with a standard liquid fertilizer.
Temperature Normal room temperatures are suitable.
Humidity This plant prefers increased humidity.

> **Decorating tip**
> *Train a Canary ivy up tall, thin bamboo canes for a bold green column.*

102

Hedera helix

ENGLISH IVY

There are many named varieties of English ivy: some have plain green leaves; others have strongly variegated leaves.

Light Grow in bright filtered light.
Water Water moderately and feed once every two weeks with a standard liquid fertilizer during the active growth period. Water sparingly during the winter.
Temperature English ivy can thrive in a broad range of temperatures, but ideally likes a temperature at around 10°C (50°F) during winter.
Humidity This plant prefers increased humidity. Stand the pot on moist pebbles and mist-spray frequently.

Decorating tip
Plant the plain green-leaved English ivy in a trough with larger plants where it will hide the surface of the potting mixture, providing attractive ground cover.

103

Hibiscus rosa-sinensis

ROSE OF CHINA

This woody-stemmed shrub is grown for its large, trumpet-shaped flowers, that may be single or double, white, yellow, orange or a very strong red.

Light Grow in direct sunlight.
Water Water moderately and feed once a week (the hibiscus is a very greedy plant) with a tomato-type liquid fertilizer (see page 133) during the active growth period. Water sparingly during the winter.
Temperature Normal room temperatures are suitable, but rest the plant at around 12°C (55°F) in winter.
Humidity The hibiscus prefers increased humidity. Stand the pot on a tray of moist pebbles.

Decorating tip
Display a hibiscus in a sunny window in a plaited palm cache pot or a square container to accentuate its oriental origins.

104
Hippeastrum hybrids
AMARYLLIS

The amaryllis is a bulbous-rooted plant that can be grown for several years in the home. It will start to grow in early spring, sending up first one or two tall flower stalks topped with several huge, trumpet-shaped flowers, then long strap-shaped leaves. The flowers may be white, pink, orange or red, either a solid colour or streaked with a paler or a darker shade of the same colour.

Light Grow the plant in direct sunlight during the active growth period. During summer, it can stand out of doors in full sun; this usually ensures the following year's blooms.

Light is unimportant to the amaryllis during the dormant winter period.

Water Water sparingly a bulb that is just starting to grow but gradually increase the amount given as growth gets under way. Water moderately and feed once every two weeks with a standard liquid fertilizer during the summer. Switch to a tomato-type liquid fertilizer (see page 133) in midsummer to help ripen the bulb and build up the next season's flowers. Stop feeding and watering when the leaves start to turn yellow in the autumn.

Temperature Warmth is needed to start the bulb growing but cool temperatures are best during the actual flowering period as this prolongs the life of the flowers. During the winter rest period the ideal temperature is around 12°C (55°F).

Humidity The amaryllis is happy in dry air.

Life cycle of an amaryllis

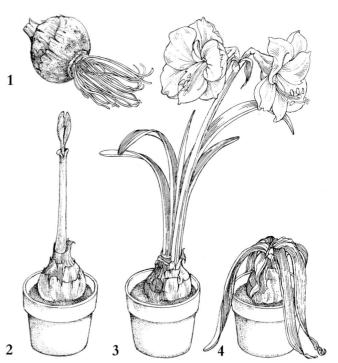

1 In winter the amaryllis has a dormant period as a dry bulb.

2 In early spring the bulb produces one or two tall flower stalks.

3 Several long leaves develop and flowers are produced.

4 In autumn the leaves and flower stalks turn yellow and then die down for winter.

Decorating tip
Make the most of these beautiful but short-lived flowers by standing the pot in a prominent position, such as in the lounge or well-lit entrance hall, where the plant can be seen and enjoyed for much of the day.

105

Howea belmoreana

KENTIA PALM

This palm, with its gracefully arching fronds, can be bought either as a small plant or as a large specimen. It has a deserved reputation for being able to grow under difficult indoor conditions, but it is really only seen at its best when it is well treated. The long leaf stalks give this plant an open, airy look. Indoors it may eventually reach 2 m (6½ ft) tall. As the howea grows older, its stem forms a short trunk that thickens at the base.

Light The kentia palm does best in bright filtered light but can be grown in places with lower light levels for relatively short periods. Prolonged periods of insufficient light, however, result in growth slowing and even stopping.

Water Water plentifully, so as to keep the potting mixture thoroughly moist, and feed once every two weeks with a standard liquid fertilizer during the active growth period. Water sparingly during the winter, giving only enough water to stop the potting mixture drying out.

Temperature This plant grows well in most normal room temperatures, but it will not tolerate the cold. Temperatures below 12°C (55°F) will result in the frond tips turning brown and shrivelling.

Humidity This plant will tolerate dry air, but if growing the plant in a warm room increase the humidity by standing the pot on a generous-sized tray filled with moist pebbles. Mist-spray the foliage frequently to discourage red spider mites that are active in dry air in warm rooms. To wash dust off the fronds, stand the plant under a cool indoor shower, or, in summer, stand the pot outside in gentle rain. Do not use a commercial leaf-cleaning product, as this may damage the fronds.

Extra point A howea prefers its roots to be confined and grows best in a pot that appears to be too small for it. Repot a plant only every two or three years in late spring, using a soil-based potting mixture. When the maximum pot size has been reached, give the plant an annual top-dressing. Make sure that the potting mixture is pressed down firmly around the roots.

Decorating tip
Give this palm plenty of space in which to grow and develop to its full size. Display it on a small plant stand in the corner of a room or window recess, where it will receive plenty of light.

Cleaning the fronds *A quick and easy method of washing dust off the fronds of a howea is to stand the plant under a tepid shower for a few minutes.*

106

Hoya bella

MINIATURE WAX PLANT

This trailing plant is best grown in a hanging basket. Its flowers appear in summer and are sweetly scented.

Light Grow in direct sunlight. Some three to four hours of sunlight a day are needed to ensure flowering.

Water Water moderately and feed once every two weeks with a tomato-type liquid fertilizer (see page 133) during the active growth period. Water very sparingly during winter.

Temperature Normal room temperatures are suitable.

Humidity This plant needs high humidity. Flowerbuds turn yellow and fall if the air is too dry. Stand the pot on moist pebbles and mist-spray the plant frequently, particularly around flowering time.

Extra point As the flowers fade and die, carefully pick them off the plant, leaving the flower spurs intact, as these will continue to produce more flowers each year if undamaged.

Decorating tip
Plant a hoya in a small hanging basket in a conservatory or sunny room where the sweetly scented flowers will be noticed and enjoyed.

107

Hoya carnosa

WAX PLANT

The wax plant is a strong-growing climber that grows by twining itself around a support. Its flower clusters appear in summer. There are two varieties of this plant: *H.c.* 'Variegata' whose leaves are edged with creamy-white, and *H.c.* 'Exotica' that has a yellow stripe down each leaf.

Light Grow in direct sunlight. This is essential for free flowering.

Water Water moderately and feed with a tomato-type liquid fertilizer (see page 133) once every two weeks from early spring to mid-autumn. Water sparingly during the winter.

Temperature Normal room temperatures are suitable.

Humidity This plant needs high humidity. Stand the pot on a tray filled with moist pebbles.

Decorating tip
Train a hoya around a hoop of stout wire pushed into the potting mixture. Stand the pot on a sunny window-sill.

108

Hypoestes phyllostachya

POLKA DOT PLANT

The hypoestes is usually grown for its attractive pink-spotted leaves. The plant does produce flowers but these are small and rather dull.

Light Grow this plant in bright filtered sunlight from early spring to late autumn but move it to a sunny position for the winter. In poor light, a plant loses its strong spotting and its stems grow leggy.
Water Water moderately and feed once every two weeks with a standard liquid fertilizer during the active growth period. Water sparingly in the winter rest period.
Temperature Normal room temperatures are suitable.
Humidity This plant benefits from increased humidity. Stand the pot on a tray of moist pebbles.
Extra points Nip out the growing points frequently to encourage bushy growth. Replace this plant annually.

Decorating tip
Arrange several young hypoestes plants together in a simple bowl or dish and display this on a low table or desk top where the decorative foliage can be seen close up.

109

Impatiens wallerana hybrids

BUSY LIZZIE

Modern busy Lizzie hybrids are neat, bushy plants that can be in flower throughout most of the year. Flower colour may be white, pink, orange, red or purple, and some are striped or streaked with another colour. The leaves may be speckled with red spots on their undersides. Some new hybrids (New Guinea hybrids) have very large flowers and decorative and strongly variegated leaves.

Light Grow this plant in bright filtered light where it will flower for most of the year, but be careful to avoid hot, direct sunlight.
Water The busy Lizzie is a thirsty plant; water moderately and feed once every two weeks with a standard liquid fertilizer for most of the year. Stop feeding and water sparingly during any short rest period. Never let the potting mixture dry out completely, however, or the plant's leaves will be lost.
Temperature Normal room temperatures are suitable, with a minimum of 12°C (55°F).
Humidity This plant benefits from increased humidity in a warm room. Stand the pot on a tray filled with moist pebbles and mist-spray frequently. This will also discourage red spider mites that can attack this plant in dry air.
Extra points New plants are normally grown from seed but any particularly attractive form can be increased by taking tip cuttings. Cuttings are best taken in late spring or early summer. Root a tip cutting 4-7 cm (2-3 in) long in either water or rooting mixture.

Decorating tip
Mass a few busy Lizzies, either the same colour, or a combination of different colours, together in a simple wicker basket and display this in a sunny window for a colourful year-round display.

110

Iresine herbstii
BLOODLEAF

The striking red leaves of this plant give it its popular name. Bloodleaf is a shrubby plant, rarely growing taller than 45 cm (18 in) high.

Light Grow in direct sunlight.
Water Water plentifully and feed with a standard liquid fertilizer once every two weeks from early spring to autumn. Water sparingly in winter.
Temperature Normal room temperatures are suitable.
Humidity High humidity is essential or the leaf tips and edges will turn brown. Stand the pot on a tray of moist pebbles.

Decorating tip
Grow several bloodleaf plants together on a window-sill, where the light will shine through the red leaves making a bold splash of colour.

111

Jasminum polyanthum
JASMINE

This spring and early summer-flowering jasmine is a strong-growing climber that twines round a support. Its flowers are pink in bud but open up pure white and are beautifully scented. Regular annual pruning is essential to prevent the plant becoming straggly and untidy.

Light Grow this plant in direct sunlight. This ensures free flowering and tight growth.
Water Water plentifully and feed once every two weeks with a standard liquid fertilizer during the active growth period. Water moderately during the winter.
Temperature This plant prefers relatively cool conditions, ideally at 12-15°C (55-60° F). This will prolong the flowering season and extend the life of each flower.
Humidity Jasmine is tolerant of quite dry air but benefits from increased humidity, to discourage red spider mites that are liable to attack. Mist-spray frequently.
Extra points Jasmine can be propagated easily from tip cuttings taken in summer or early autumn. To encourage a young plant to develop several stems, pinch out the main growing point when the stem is about 30 cm (1 ft) long.

Decorating tip

A jasmine plant flowers best when its stems are trained horizontally. Grow it around a wire hoop or small bamboo trellis support pushed into the potting mixture. Display the plant in a large sunny window for the best effect.

112

Justicia brandegeana

SHRIMP PLANT

This plant was known as *Beloperone guttata* for many years. It earned its popular name from its flower-heads that are very shrimp-like in appearance.

Light Grow in direct sunlight throughout the year.
Water Water moderately and feed once every two weeks with a standard liquid fertilizer during the active growth period. Water sparingly during the winter.
Temperature Normal room temperatures are suitable.
Humidity This plant is tolerant of relatively dry air.
Extra point When at its best, this plant is bushy and carries many flower-heads. Pinch out the growing tips regularly to encourage side branches to develop.

Decorating tip
This plant has soft and muted colours that can be accentuated by growing several young plants together.

113

Kalanchoe blossfeldiana hybrids

FLAMING KATY

The vibrant coloured flowers of this plant are very long lasting, making it a useful flowering plant for growing indoors. It is a temporary plant (see page 142) and should be thrown away when the flowers cease to be produced.

Light Grow this plant in direct sunlight.
Water Water sparingly throughout the year. A plant is liable to rot at the base if it is overwatered. This temporary plant does not need feeding.
Temperature Normal room temperatures are suitable.
Humidity This plant thrives in dry air.

Decorating tip
Flaming Katy adds a splash of intense colour in a mixed planting arrangement.

114

Kalanchoe marmorata

PEN WIPER PLANT

Although it occasionally produces white flowers, this kalanchoe is mostly prized for its fleshy leaves covered with purplish-brown spots.

Light Grow in direct sunlight.
Water Water moderately and feed once every two or three weeks with a standard liquid fertilizer during the active growth period. Water sparingly during winter.
Temperature Normal room temperatures are suitable with a winter rest at around 10–12°C (50–55°F).
Humidity This plant is happy in relatively dry air.

Decorating tip
With its decorative foliage, this plant is best appreciated close up. Stand it on a kitchen window-sill or sunny shelf.

115

Kalanchoe 'Tessa'

This hybrid kalanchoe produces slender stems, on the end of which hang striking bell-shaped flowers in a pink or soft apricot colour. The flowers appear mainly in spring but some can still be found in summer.

Light Grow in direct sunlight throughout the year.
Water Water moderately, and feed once every two weeks with a standard liquid fertilizer whilst plants are in bud and in flower. Water sparingly during the winter, just enough to prevent the potting mixture drying out.
Temperature Normal room temperatures are suitable.
Humidity This kalanchoe benefits from increased humidity if being grown in a warm room. Stand the pot on a tray of moist pebbles and mist-spray the foliage regularly.

Decorating tip
This kalanchoe is one of the best flowering plants for displaying in a hanging basket. Plant up three or more rooted cuttings in a basket and hang this in a sunny window. The leaves and stems are decorative even without the flowers, but the plant becomes most striking when its flowers appear.

116

Kalanchoe tomentosa

PUSSY EARS

The leaves of this kalanchoe are densely covered with silvery hairs and tipped with a rusty-brown colour.

Light Grow in direct sunlight.
Water Water sparingly and feed once every two weeks with a standard liquid fertilizer during the active growth period. Water very sparingly during winter.
Temperature Normal room temperatures are suitable.
Humidity This plant likes dry air.

Decorating tip
Grow this kalanchoe in a small dish garden along with smooth-leaved plants for an unusual contrast in leaf texture.

117

Lithops lesliei
LIVING STONES

Living stones is an unusual plant consisting of two fleshy leaves packed closely together. At flowering time (usually late summer or early autumn), a single daisy-like flower, 2.5 cm (1 in) across, appears from the crease between the leaves. The plant forms clumps and several flowers can appear on a clump at the same time.

Light Grow in direct sunlight.
Water Water sparingly from early spring until the flowers fade. Keep the potting mixture dry in winter (during this time the old leaves shrivel and are replaced by a new pair). There is no need to feed this plant.
Temperature Normal room temperatures are suitable, with a winter temperature of 10°C (50°F).
Humidity This plant likes dry air and requires no extra humidity.

Decorating tip
Plant the lithops in a small, shallow terracotta pan, and cover the surface of the potting mixture with stones of a similar colouring to the lithops, to simulate their native habitat.

118

Livistona chinensis
CHINESE FAN PALM

The Chinese fan palm is slow-growing, developing into a small shrub 180 cm (6 ft) tall over many years. As with all palms, it is vital to ensure that the growing point is not damaged in any way. If it is, no new fronds can develop.

Light Grow in bright filtered light.
Water Water moderately and feed once every two weeks with a standard liquid fertilizer during the active growth period. Water sparingly during winter.
Temperature This plant is tolerant of a wide range of temperatures, with a winter minimum of 7°C (45°F).
Humidity This plant benefits from extra humidity if temperatures climb. Stand the pot on a large tray of moist pebbles and mist-spray the plant frequently.

Decorating tip
Stand a livistona on the floor in a prominent position where the thin leaf sections of the fan-shaped fronds can be viewed from all angles.

119

Lobivia hertrichiana
COB CACTUS

The most striking feature of this cactus is its large scarlet flowers that appear in early summer. The decorative spines provide interest all year.

Light Grow in direct sunlight.
Water Water moderately and feed once every two weeks with a tomato-type liquid fertilizer (see page 133) from early spring to mid-autumn. Water sparingly during the winter.
Temperature The cob cactus will grow in normal room temperatures for most of the year, but it needs a winter rest at around 10°C (50°F).
Humidity This cactus likes dry air.

Decorating tip
Grow the cob cactus in a shallow pan or half-pot on a sunny desk top or shelf, where its colourful, cup-shaped flowers can be appreciated.

120

Mammillaria zeilmanniana

ROSE PINCUSHIO·N

The clump-forming mammillaria produces many small purplish-red flowers in the summer.

Light Grow in direct sunlight.
Water Water moderately and feed with a tomato-type liquid fertilizer (see page 133) once a month during the active growth period. In winter water sparingly.
Temperature Normal room temperatures are suitable, but the plant must rest in winter at around 10°C (50°F) to ensure that it flowers the following year.
Humidity This plant tolerates dry air and needs no extra humidity.

Decorating tip
Place a mammillaria on a sunny window-sill where it will quickly form a clump and make a striking feature in the summer, when it will be covered with dozens of purplish-red flowers.

121

Maranta leuconeura erythroneura

PRAYER PLANT

The decorative leaves of this plant display prominent red vein markings on the upper surfaces and are deep purple underneath. Flowers are produced but they are insignificant. Although the maranta can be grown up a short moss pole or small trellis, it is usually low and spreading. This plant gets its common name from the way its leaves fold together at night.

Light Grow the plant in medium light during most of the year but move it to bright filtered light during the winter. In very bright light the leaves fade and develop brown edges.
Water Water plentifully and feed with a standard liquid fertilizer once every two weeks throughout the active growth period. Water moderately during the winter rest period. Always allow the potting mixture to dry out a little between applications, but never let the mixture dry out completely.
Temperature Normal room temperatures are suitable for this plant. A minimum temperature of 15°C (60°F) is essential.

Humidity This tropical rainforest plant thrives in high humidity. If growing the plant in a warm room, stand the pot on a tray filled with damp pebbles and mist-spray the plant regularly. Use rainwater if possible, as this does not mark the leaves.
Extra point A maranta can be propagated by dividing a large clump in spring or by taking cuttings in summer (see page 136). Use a soil-based potting mixture.

Decorating tip
Plant two or three young plants in one pot and then train them up a short, moist moss-covered pole. Mist-spray the pole regularly to encourage the plant's roots to grow into the moss.

122

Mikania ternata

PLUSH VINE

This climbing plant has purplish-grey, lobed leaves that are covered in soft hairs when young. Its stems, when supported, can reach up to 1 m (3-4 ft) high.

Light Grow the plant in bright filtered light all year.
Water Water moderately. Feed with a standard liquid fertilizer once every two weeks during the active growth period.
Temperature The plush vine thrives in normal room temperatures with a minimum of 12°C (55°F) in winter.
Humidity This plant enjoys high humidity. Stand the pot on a tray of moist pebbles and mist-spray the plant on very hot days.

Decorating tip
This climbing plant can also be allowed to trail. Plant it in a trough or square planter where its rambling stems will spill and trail over the edges and soften the hard outline of the container.

123

Monstera deliciosa

SWISS CHEESE PLANT

This large-leaved, long-stalked climber makes a dramatic indoor plant. Small and large monsteras are available, but a mature plant displays the deepest cut edges.

Light Grow the plant in bright filtered light.
Water Water moderately, and feed with a standard liquid fertilizer once every two weeks during the active growth period.
Temperature Normal room temperatures are suitable, with a minimum of 12°C (55°F) in winter.
Humidity This plant prefers increased humidity. Stand it on moist pebbles and mist-spray frequently.
Extra point Tuck any long aerial roots into the potting mixture, so that they can take up nutrients.

Decorating tip
When space permits, train a monstera up a stout support, and position this in a bright corner of a room.

124

Myrtus communis

MYRTLE

Myrtle is grown for its decorative, sweetly-scented leaves and its striking, white or pale pink scented flowers that are produced in summer.

Light Grow in direct sunlight.
Water Water plentifully during the active growth period and moderately during the winter rest period. Feed only a well-established plant with a standard liquid fertilizer once every two weeks from early spring through to late summer.
Temperature This plant likes warmth for most of the year and a winter rest at around 7°C (45°F).
Humidity The myrtle is able to withstand dry air.
Extra point This plant is happiest out of doors during the summer; stand it in a sheltered but sunny spot.

Decorating tip
Display one or two myrtle shrubs in a cool but brightly-lit conservatory where their fragrance can be enjoyed without being overpowering.

125

Neoregelia carolinae 'Tricolor'

BLUSHING BROMELIAD

The name, blushing bromeliad, comes from the way that the centre of the rosette of leaves flushes red at the time of flowering. A thick, stemless flower-head grows in the cup-like centre of the leaves and produces small white or blue flowers just clear of the waterline. Once a rosette of leaves has flowered, it dies.

Light Grow in direct sunlight.
Water Water moderately and feed once every two weeks with half-strength standard liquid fertilizer from early spring to mid-autumn. Splash feed and water over the leaves. Water sparingly during the winter. Keep the centre of the rosette of leaves topped up with fresh water.
Temperature Normal room temperatures are suitable.
Humidity This plant does not demand moist air.

Decorating tip
Stand the blushing bromeliad on a low table once it has started to "blush", so you can look down on to the red centre and rosy flush that extends through most of the rosette of leaves.

126

Nephrolepis exaltata

SWORD FERN

Only varieties of this plant are grown, and the original species is not seen. The frond sections grow in two rows, one on either side of a wiry midrib. They may be undulating, with frilled or crimped edges, and can grow up to 90-150 cm (3-5 ft) long.

Light Grow this plant in bright filtered light throughout the year.
Water Water plentifully and feed actively growing plants once every two weeks with a standard liquid fertilizer. Water the plant moderately during the winter.
Temperature Normal room temperatures are suitable.
Humidity As temperatures climb, it is necessary to increase the level of humidity or the frond tips and segments will turn brown. Stand the pot on a tray of moist pebbles and mist-spray regularly.

Decorating tip
The gracefully arching fronds of this fern make it perfect for displaying on a raised plant stand or pedestal. It will suit both modern and period interiors.

127

Nerium oleander

OLEANDER

This woody-stemmed shrub is grown for its clusters of pink flowers. There are varieties with yellow, orange, red and white flowers.

Light This plant requires a really bright sunny position.
Water Water moderately throughout the year. Feed once every two weeks with a standard liquid fertilizer during spring and summer.
Temperature The oleander is tolerant of a wide range of temperatures, but needs a winter minimum temperature of 7°C (45°F).
Humidity This plant likes dry air.
Extra point Most parts of this plant are poisonous, so avoid placing an oleander where very young children can reach it.

Decorating tip
As the oleander will not object to a certain amount of neglect and an occasional draught, an ideal position to grow it is a cool porch or well-lit entrance hall. Here there will be enough sunlight to bring the plant into flower.

128

Nertera granadensis

BEAD PLANT

The bead plant is grown for its decorative, bright orange berries that appear on the plant in late summer and remain for several months. Although this plant can be kept for a second year, this is rather difficult, and most indoor gardeners treat it as a temporary house plant (see page 142), to be thrown away when the berries lose their appeal.

Light Grow this plant in direct sunlight at all times.
Water Water a bead plant moderately, allowing some drying out of the potting mixture between applications, but never let the mixture dry out completely. There is no need to feed this plant.
Temperature Normal room temperatures are suitable.

Humidity Herein lies one of the secrets of success in growing the bead plant. High humidity is essential. Increase the level of humidity by standing the pot on a tray of moist pebbles and mist-spraying the plant frequently.

Decorating tip
The charm of this plant is its low-growing, creeping habit and its bright orange berries; it makes a very colourful table decoration. For an effective display, stand the pot on a wide dish filled with pretty pebbles. These will add interest as well as helping to increase the humidity. The plant will eventually creep over the edge of its pot and spill down the sides.

129

Nidularium fulgens

This shiny-leaved bromeliad is coloured a fresh light green. The stumpy flower-head has red bracts and violet-blue flowers. Although the flowers are short-lived, the flower-head remains decorative for several weeks. Once the rosette of leaves has flowered, it dies.

Light Grow in bright filtered light.
Water Water moderately at all times and feed once every two weeks with half-strength standard liquid fertilizer during the active growth period. Splash water and feed over the leaves as well as on the potting mixture. Keep the central cup filled with fresh water until flowering time.
Temperature Normal room temperatures are suitable, with a winter minimum of 12°C (55°F).
Humidity This plant needs high humidity. Stand the pot on moist pebbles and mist-spray frequently.

Decorating tip
Grow this plant on its own, on a low table or other surface, where it can be viewed from above and its red centre clearly appreciated.

130

Nidularium innocentii

BIRD'S NEST BROMELIAD

This nidularium has finely toothed leaves that are deep green, overlaid with a metallic purple-brown. The leaf undersides are glossy and coloured wine red. In autumn orange-red bracts surround the white flowers on a slightly raised flower-head. Once the nidularium has flowered the rosette of leaves then dies.

Light Grow this plant in bright filtered light all year.
Water Water moderately throughout the year. Feed once every two weeks with half-strength standard liquid fertilizer during the active growth period. Keep the central cup filled with fresh water until flowering time. Splash water and feed over the leaves as well as on the potting mixture.
Temperature Normal room temperatures are suitable, with a winter minimum of 12°C (55°F).
Humidity A high level is essential; stand the pot on a tray of moist pebbles and mist-spray frequently.

Decorating tip
This plant is greatly prized for its unique metallic look, and can be effectively displayed on a tall plant stand. When the colourful bracts appear, move the plant to a lower level so the attractive flower-head can be seen.

131

Oplismenus hirtellus 'Variegatus'

RIBBON GRASS

Ribbon grass looks like a narrow and thin-leaved tradescantia. It is, however, a very decorative grass.

Light Grow in direct sunlight.
Water Water plentifully and feed with a standard liquid fertilizer once a month during the active growth period. Water sparingly in winter.
Temperature Ribbon grass grows well in a wide range of temperatures, but needs a temperature in winter of at least 12°C (55°F).
Humidity This plant will tolerate dry air, but benefits from increased humidity in a warm room.
Extra point As a plant grows older, it tends to lose some of its lower (older) leaves and is best discarded.

Decorating tip
Display ribbon grass in a hanging basket in a brightly lit window where the delicate leaves will show to their best advantage.

132

Opuntia microdasys

PRICKLY PEAR

This cactus makes a very suitable house plant as it rarely grows taller than 30 cm (1 ft) high. It is spineless but clusters of golden yellow, prickly glochids (see page 142) grow evenly over the green, oval segments. These can penetrate the skin if handled.

Light Grow in direct sunlight.
Water Water moderately and feed every two weeks with a tomato-type liquid fertilizer (see page 133) during spring and summer. Water sparingly during winter.
Temperature Normal room temperatures are suitable with a winter minimum of 10°C (50°F).
Humidity This plant is unaffected by dry air and requires no extra humidity.
Extra point When handling the plant, it is advisable to wrap a stout fold of paper around it to protect your hands from the prickles.

Decorating tip
Plant an opuntia in a small cactus garden, where it will add height and interest. Display this on a sunny window-sill where it cannot be accidentally brushed against.

133

Pachyphytum oviferum

MOONSTONES

This fleshy-leaved succulent rarely grows taller than 15 cm (6 in) high. It is grown mainly for its attractive greyish leaves that are covered with a white "bloom". Bright red flowers are occasionally produced.

Light Grow in direct sunlight throughout the year.
Water Water moderately during the active growth period and sparingly during the winter to stop or slow down growth. It is not necessary to feed the pachyphytum.
Temperature Normal room temperatures are suitable for the pachyphytum. An ideal winter temperature (when the plant is dryish at the roots) is 10-15°C (50-60°F).
Humidity This plant is unaffected by dry air and requires no extra humidity.

Decorating tip
Display the pachyphytum on its own in a shallow terracotta pan or half-pot on a sunny window-sill, where it can be seen at close quarters. Be careful not to handle the plant or the "bloom" will be spoiled.

PALMS

There are two basic types of palm – feathery palms and fan palms. Palm leaves are normally called fronds and they are made up of many segments or leaflets. Feathery palms have segments that are arranged in two rows, one on either side of a stout midrib. The leaflets may be stiff and even prickly or they may be soft and pliable. Fan palms develop stout frond stalks and all the segments grow from a common point, arranged in a fan-like group.

Palms grow from one growing point which is situated in the middle of a group of leaves. It is protected by unopened fronds, but, if damaged, it is not replaced. Although old and damaged leaves can be removed from palms, a palm should not be cut down, as this would damage the growing point.

Some palms develop offsets around the base and form clumps; others remain as solitary plants. After a number of years, a trunk may develop on some palms, but this is uncommon on palms grown indoors.

151
Phoenix roebelenii
Pygmy date palm

117
Livistona chinensis
Chinese fan palm

42
Caryota mitis
Fishtail palm

150
Phoenix canariensis
Canary date palm

166
Rhapis excelsa
Lady palm

49
Chamaerops humilis
European fan palm

Cultivation

Most palms are tropical or sub-tropical in origin and prefer bright light and warm temperatures. They need to be watered plentifully but they do not require high humidity. However, it is best to stand a palm on a tray of moist pebbles when growing it in a warm room.

All palms resent root disturbance and should only be repotted and moved on into the next size pot every few years when they really need it.

51
Chrysalidocarpus lutescens
Golden-feather palm

48
Chamaedorea elegans
Parlour palm

105
Howea belmoreana
Kentia palm

134

Pandanus veitchii

SCREW PINE

The long, leathery leaves of this plant are arranged in a spiral, giving it its common name. They are striped and edged with very fine spines.

Light Grow in direct sunlight.
Water Water plentifully and feed once every two weeks with a standard liquid fertilizer during the active growth period. Water sparingly during winter.
Temperature Normal room temperatures are ideal, with a winter minimum of 12°C (55°F).
Humidity This plant benefits from increased humidity. Stand the pot on a tray of moist pebbles.
Extra point When the plant is a few years old, it sends out prop-like roots from the bottom of its leaves that partially lift the plant out of the potting mixture in the pot.

Decorating tip
With its large, gracefully arching leaves, this plant is best displayed on a pedestal or tall plant stand, in a sunny corner of the living room.

135

Passiflora caerulea

PASSION FLOWER

The passion flower has very decorative and unusual flowers and is relatively easy to grow. It fastens on to supports with wiry tendrils. A plant flowers when it is quite young and needs annual pruning.

Light Grow in direct sunlight.
Water Water plentifully and feed once every two weeks with a standard liquid fertilizer during the active growth period. Water sparingly in the winter to encourage a rest period.
Temperature This plant is frost hardy but will grow well in a warm room. It must, however, have a cool winter rest period, ideally at a temperature around 10°C (50°F).
Humidity This plant needs high humidity. Stand the pot on moist pebbles and mist-spray frequently.
Extra point Prune the plant in spring by taking out any over-long, old stems and cutting all younger stems back to 10-15 cm (4-6 in).

Decorating tip
Train a passion flower around a double hoop of stout cane or wire pushed into the potting mixture. Show it off on a small table in a window recess.

136

Pelargonium crispum 'Variegatum'

LEMON GERANIUM

This geranium is grown for its decorative and scented leaves that have crimped and curled edges and yellow markings.

Light Grow in direct sunlight.
Water Water moderately and feed once every two weeks with a tomato-type liquid fertilizer (see page 133) during the active growth period. Water sparingly during the winter.
Temperature This plant is tolerant of a wide range of temperatures, with a winter minimum of 10°C (50°F).
Humidity This geranium is unaffected by dry air.

Decorating tip

This plant has a pretty old-fashioned feel and would suit a more informal room. Stand it on a ledge or table where you can brush against it to release its deliciously fresh scent.

137

Pelargonium domesticum hybrids

REGAL GERANIUM

This shrubby pelargonium flowers mainly in spring and early summer. It produces very large flower-heads that sometimes hide most of the foliage; the flowers can be white, pink, red or shades of purple, sometimes striped or marked with another colour.

Light Grow in direct sunlight throughout the year.
Water Water moderately and feed once every two weeks with a tomato-type liquid fertilizer (see page 133) during the active growth period. Water sparingly during the winter.
Temperature Normal room temperatures are suitable but ideally rest the plant at around 10°C (50°F) in the winter months.
Humidity This plant is tolerant of dry air and needs no extra humidity.
Extra point When the flowering stops, cut away the dead flowers and prune the plant back by at least half. Rest the plant for about a month, then repot and grow on as above.

Decorating tip

For a bold display, group several pelargoniums together, either on a window-sill, or on a table top, ensuring that their colours complement each other.

138

Pelargonium hortorum hybrids

ZONAL GERANIUM

The zonal geranium has a distinctive ball-shaped flower-head and vibrant flowers. Some forms have a dark circular zone on their leaves.

Light Grow in bright direct sunlight.
Water Water moderately and feed once every two weeks with a tomato-type liquid fertilizer (see page 133) during the active growth period. Water sparingly in winter.
Temperature Normal room temperatures are suitable for most of the year, with a rest in winter at around 10°C (50°F).
Humidity This plant is unaffected by dry air and needs no extra humidity.
Extra point In really bright light a zonal geranium will continue to flower during the winter, but it is best to rest it by reducing its watering.

Decorating tip
Stand a pair of zonal geraniums on the window-sill of a sunny window and train them around the framework.

139

Pelargonium peltatum hybrids

IVY-LEAVED GERANIUM

The ivy-shaped leaves and the trailing habit of growth give this plant its common name. Its flowers may be white, pink, red or shades of mauve and they appear mainly in spring. A few plants have variegated leaves.

Light Grow in direct sunlight.
Water Water moderately and feed once every two weeks with a tomato-type liquid fertilizer (see page 133) from spring to autumn. Water sparingly in winter. Do not overwater, or rot may set in.
Temperature Normal room temperatures are suitable with a winter minimum of 10°C (50°F).
Humidity This plant is content in dry air and needs no extra humidity.

Decorating tip
An ivy-leaved geranium looks splendid in a hanging basket. Plant several rooted cuttings in a basket in early spring and hang it in a sunny window. The plant will soon develop into a lovely display.

140

Pellaea rotundifolia

BUTTON FERN

The button fern is unusual in that it has a spreading rather than upright habit, unlike other ferns. Its fronds rarely exceed 30 cm (1 ft) long and grow on virtually horizontal, wiry stems.

Light Grow this fern in medium light, avoiding direct sun.
Water Water plentifully from spring to autumn so the mixture is thoroughly moist. If the temperature is cooler in winter, water sparingly, giving just enough to moisten the mixture. Feed with a standard liquid fertilizer once every two weeks during the active growth period.
Temperature The button fern is tolerant of a wide range of temperatures but needs a winter minimum of 10°C (50°F).
Humidity Unlike most ferns this plant is able to grow well in dry air, but it does benefit from increased humidity. Mist-spray the foliage at higher temperatures.

Decorating tip
This plant is excellent for growing as ground cover in a trough and under larger spreading plants, where its arching fronds will soften the edges of the container.

141

Pentas lanceolata

EGYPTIAN STAR CLUSTER

The small flowers of the pentas grow in a dense cluster and may be white, pink, lilac or a beautiful shade of red. Each cluster of flowers lasts for several weeks.

Light Grow this plant in direct sunlight or very bright filtered light. Insufficient light results in leggy growth and poor flowering.
Water Water moderately and feed once every two weeks with a standard liquid fertilizer during spring, summer and autumn. Water sparingly in winter.
Temperature The pentas loves warmth. Provide a winter minimum temperature of 15°C (60°F).
Humidity This plant prefers relatively humid air.

Decorating tip
This is a very simple plant that fits in best with traditional interiors. Treat it like a cottage plant by displaying it in a simple wicker basket, or grouping several together for a colourful table top display.

142

Peperomia argyreia

WATERMELON PEPEROMIA

This plant was called *P. sandersii* for many years. Its shiny, heart-shaped leaves are so striped that it has a three-dimensional look.

Light Grow in bright filtered light.
Water Water moderately and feed once a month with half-strength standard liquid fertilizer from spring to autumn. Water very sparingly during the winter. Overwatering is the commonest cause of failure.
Temperature The peperomia appreciates warmth. Provide a winter temperature of at least 12°C (55°F).
Humidity In a warm room this plant benefits from increased humidity. Stand the pot on moist pebbles.

Decorating tip
The alternate bands of silver and green on the peperomia's foliage are best appreciated when this plant is seen close up. Position it under a table lamp during the evening to give the plant extra light.

143

Peperomia caperata

EMERALD RIPPLE

This is the best known peperomia and one prized for its corrugated leaf surface. It also regularly produces white, tail-like flower spikes.

Light Grow in bright filtered light.
Water Water moderately and feed once a month with half-strength standard liquid fertilizer from early spring to mid-autumn. Water very sparingly during the winter. Over-watering can kill the plant.
Temperature Provide warm conditions. A winter minimum of 12°C (55°F) is essential.
Humidity This plant benefits from increased humidity. Stand the pot on a tray of moist pebbles. Do not mist-spray the plant as water lodging in leaf corrugations can cause rot.

Decorating tip
Arrange this plant in a shallow bowl with other peperomias that have different leaf textures and colours, such as P. argyreia and P. magnoliifolia for interesting and subtle contrast.

144

Peperomia griseoargentea

SILVERLEAF PEPEROMIA

This peperomia can be distinguished from all the others by its heart-shaped, silvery and slightly quilted leaves. There is a variety of this peperomia, *P.g.* 'Nigra', that has almost black vein areas.

Light Grow in bright filtered light.
Water Overwatering will certainly kill this plant. Water moderately and feed once a month with half-strength standard liquid fertilizer during the active growth period. Water very sparingly during the winter.
Temperature This plant likes warmth and needs a minimum winter temperature of 12°C (55°F).
Humidity This plant benefits from increased humidity. Stand the pot on a tray of moist pebbles, but do not mist-spray as this can cause rot.

Decorating tip
Grow this peperomia with an asparagus fern to provide an interesting contrast of textures: the solid, metallic-looking peperomia leaves against the thin, spiky foliage of the asparagus fern.

145

Peperomia magnoliifolia

DESERT PRIVET

This peperomia has almost oval, very fleshy, dark green leaves. Equally popular is the variegated-leaved form, *P.m.* 'Variegata', that has large patches of a strong yellow-green colour on its leaves.

Light Grow in bright filtered light. This is essential for the variegated-leaved form, or much of the colour contrast will be lost.
Water Avoid overwatering as this can kill the plant. Water moderately and feed every month with half-strength standard liquid fertilizer during the active growth period. Water very sparingly in winter.
Temperature Normal room temperatures are suitable, with a winter minimum of 12°C (55°F).
Humidity This plant benefits from increased humidity in a warm room. Stand the pot on a tray of moist pebbles; do not mist-spray.

Decorating tip
This plant is upright growing at first but in time, mainly because of its heavy leaves, it starts to sprawl. Take advantage of this by allowing it to creep over the sides of a container, softening the hard edges.

146

Philodendron bipinnatifidum

FINGER PLANT

The finger plant does not climb (as do most philodendrons) but in time it develops a short stem and can grow to about 120 cm (4 ft) high. Its large, fingered leaves grow on long, stout stalks, making a very striking plant.

Light Grow in bright filtered light, avoiding direct sunlight, throughout the year. Insufficient light results in leggy growth and poor colour.
Water Water moderately and feed once every two weeks with a standard liquid fertilizer from early spring to late autumn. Water sparingly in winter, giving only enough to prevent the mixture from drying out.
Temperature Normal room temperatures are ideal, with a winter minimum of 12°C (55°F).
Humidity This plant needs high humidity. Stand the pot on moist pebbles and mist-spray regularly.

Decorating tip
Stand this philodendron in a large brass or smooth-textured ceramic pot in a full-length window, where its deeply cut leaves will contrast with the container, and provide a strong dramatic outline.

147

Philodendron domesticum

SPADE-LEAF

This climber with its long spade- or spear-shaped leaves can reach up to 150 cm (5 ft) tall.

Light Grow this plant in bright filtered light, avoiding hot summer sun, throughout the year.
Water Water moderately and feed once every two weeks with a standard liquid fertilizer during the active growth period. Water sparingly in the winter months.

Temperature Grow in warm temperatures, with a winter minimum of 12°C (55°F).
Humidity This plant needs high humidity. Stand the pot on moist pebbles and mist-spray frequently.

Decorating tip
Display this philodendron on its own where its bold leaves and stout leaf stalks have room to spread and be seen.

148

Philodendron erubescens

BLUSHING PHILODENDRON

The blushing philodendron has deep red stems, pink protective leaf sheaths and new leaves which are tinged red.

Light Grow in bright filtered light.
Water Water moderately and feed once every two weeks with a standard liquid fertilizer during the active growth period. Water the philodendron sparingly in winter.
Temperatures This plant enjoys warm temperatures, with a winter minimum of 12°C (55°F).
Humidity This plant needs high humidity. Stand the pot on a tray of moist pebbles.

Decorating tip
Stand this philodendron on the floor next to a brightly lit, full-length window, where the light will enhance the pink and red colouring of the leaves.

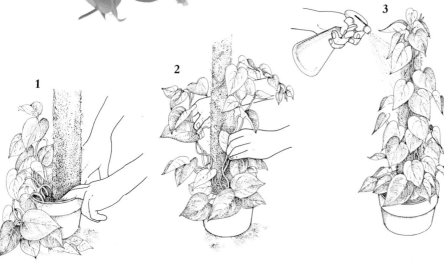

149

Philodendron scandens

SWEETHEART VINE

The sweetheart vine is the most popular and the easiest philodendron to grow. It is a climber that can reach 2 m (6½ ft) tall, although its stems can be trained around supports and seem to remain much shorter. Aerial roots are produced at every leaf axil and if they find a favourable moist contact they develop and cling to it, otherwise they wither and dry up. This philodendron is very useful for training up a moss-covered pole, but it also looks good as a trailing plant or when grown in a hanging basket.

Light Grow in bright filtered light, avoiding direct summer sun throughout the year.
Water Water moderately and feed once every two weeks with a standard liquid fertilizer during the active growth period. Water sparingly in winter.
Temperature Normal room temperatures are ideal, with a winter minimum of 12°C (55°F).
Humidity This plant needs high humidity. Stand the pot on a tray of moist pebbles and mist-spray frequently both the plant and the moss pole (if being used).

Decorating tip
Plant several small plants in one pot and train them around a moist moss-covered pole (see below). Use a potting mixture of equal parts soil-based compost and coarse peat or leafmould. At first it will be necessary to fasten the stems with string or wire to the moist moss surface, but as the aerial roots start to develop and cling to the moss, they will hold the stems secure. It is important that the moss-covered pole is mist-sprayed regularly, otherwise the fastening roots will not develop.

TRAINING UP A MOSS POLE

1 Stand the moss pole in the centre of the pot and pack potting mixture around it. Then plant several sweetheart vines in the potting mixture, and firm them in place.

2 Wind the trailing stems around the moss pole, and secure them with wire.

3 Mist-spray the foliage and the moss pole regularly. This will encourage the plant to grow aerial roots which will grow into the pole and give the plant extra support.

150

Phoenix canariensis

CANARY DATE PALM

This very popular palm produces rather prickly fronds. It is slow-growing but can reach 2 m (6 ft) tall. Eventually a short bulbous base, covered with wiry fibres, develops.

Light Grow in direct sunlight all year.
Water Water plentifully and feed once every two weeks with a standard liquid fertilizer during the active growth period. Water sparingly during the winter.
Temperature This palm is tolerant of a wide range of temperatures, but prefers a lower temperature, with a minimum of 10°C (50°F), during the winter rest period.
Humidity The Canary date palm is unworried by dry air.

Decorating tip
This large plant is very useful for growing in cool rooms, such as a porch or well-lit entrance hall, where few other house plants will thrive.

151

Phoenix roebelenii

PYGMY DATE PALM

This grand tropical date palm produces finely divided, gracefully arching fronds, and it can grow up to 1 m (3 ft) tall, with a similar spread.

Light Grow in bright filtered light.
Water Water plentifully and feed once every two weeks with a standard liquid fertilizer during the active growth period. Water more sparingly during the winter.
Temperature Normal room temperatures are suitable but they should not fall below 15°C (60°F) in winter.
Humidity This palm enjoys high humidity. Stand it on a tray filled with moist pebbles and mist-spray frequently.

Decorating tip
This is a palm that should be viewed from all sides. Display it on a pedestal or tall plant stand so that its arching fronds can be seen to their best advantage.

152

Pilea cadierei

ALUMINIUM PLANT

This is one of the easiest of the pileas to grow and one of the most attractive. Its silvery, puckered leaves are very distinctive. It is more upright than most pileas but rarely grows taller than 25 cm (10 in) high.

Light Grow in medium light.
Water Water moderately and feed once every two weeks with a standard liquid fertilizer during the active growth period. Water sparingly during the winter.
Temperature This plant enjoys warmth and will not tolerate temperatures below 12°C (55°F).
Humidity High humidity is essential. Stand the pot on a tray of moist pebbles.

Decorating tip
For a lovely blend of subtle colours and contrasting leaf textures, grow this plant amongst other pileas, such as P. spruceana 'Norfolk', in a small bowl. Each plant will complement its neighbour, and all will thrive because of their similar needs and close proximity.

153

Pilea spruceana 'Norfolk'

The charm of this pilea is its pink-tinged, metallic-looking leaves that are best appreciated at close quarters.

Light Grow in medium light during spring and summer but move to bright filtered light for the winter months.
Water Water moderately and feed once every two weeks with a standard liquid fertilizer during the active growth period. Water sparingly during the winter.
Temperature This plant grows well in a warm room, with a winter minimum of 12°C (55°F).
Humidity This pilea needs high humidity. Stand the pot on a tray of moist pebbles and mist-spray the foliage occasionally.

Decorating tip
Grow this pilea in a terrarium or bottle garden on a low table, where you can look down on the decorative rosettes of leaves.

154

Piper crocatum

ORNAMENTAL PEPPER

This wiry-stemmed climbing plant is grown for its heart-shaped leaves that are deep olive green with metallic, silvery vein areas above, and deep purple underneath.

Light Grow in bright filtered light.
Water Water moderately throughout the year. Feed once every two weeks with a standard liquid fertilizer whilst growth is active.
Temperature This pepper loves warmth and needs a winter minimum of 15°C (60°F).
Humidity This plant needs high humidity. Stand the pot on a tray of moist pebbles and mist-spray the foliage frequently.

Decorating tip
Train the stems of the pepper plant up several thin canes to form a column of colourful foliage and stand it in a brightly lit window. The deep purple undersides of the leaves will give the plant a rosy hue.

155

Platycerium bifurcatum

STAGHORN FERN

This very unusual looking fern grows two distinct kinds of frond. The decorative and prominent fronds are shaped like a stag's antlers; they carry spores on their undersides and are called the fertile fronds. The second type of frond is the flat sterile frond. This holds the fern to its support.

Light Grow in bright filtered light.
Water During the active growth period a platycerium likes to be thoroughly watered and then allowed to become *almost* completely dry before being watered again. This is best done by soaking it in a bowl of water. Feed the plant two or three times during the summer with a standard liquid fertilizer added to the water in the bowl. In the winter give it just a brief dip in water.
Temperature Normal room temperatures are suitable.
Humidity High humidity is vital for a platycerium. Mist-spray a plant that is grown on bark or wood daily, and mist-spray its base as well.

Decorating tip
Fix a platycerium to a piece of cork bark and hang this on a wall to simulate its natural environment, where it grows on tree trunks and limbs. Remember to mist-spray the moss, fronds and base frequently and handle the plant very carefully until the sterile frond has a firm hold on the base.

Attaching a platycerium to bark

1 *Wrap the roots in a moist mixture of sphagnum moss and coarse peat.*

2 *Using string, tie the moss-wrapped rootball to a piece of cork bark.*

3 *Hang the platycerium from a hook attached to the wall or ceiling.*

156

Plectranthus oertendahlii

CANDLE PLANT

This trailing plant can grow up to 1 m (3 ft) long. Its leaves are dark green with silvery vein markings above and deep purple underneath. Pale lavender flowers are produced in short spikes; they are not particularly attractive and are best nipped out.

Light Grow this plant in direct sunlight throughout the year. Inadequate light results in the plant becoming leggy and unattractive.
Water Water plentifully and feed with a standard liquid fertilizer once every two weeks throughout the active growth period. Water moderately during the winter.
Temperature This plant will thrive in normal room temperatures, with a minimum temperature of 12°C (55°F) in the winter.
Humidity This plant prefers extra humidity. Stand the pot on a tray filled with moist pebbles.

Decorating tip
Display the plant in a hanging basket in a brightly-lit window, where its deep purple leaf veins will show to their best advantage.

157

Plumbago auriculata

CAPE LEADWORT

The plumbago is a shrubby plant, the trailing stems of which are best trained around wire or cane hoops or up a framework pushed into the potting mixture. The flowers are pale blue.

Light Grow in direct sunlight.
Water Water plentifully and feed with a standard liquid fertilizer once every two weeks from spring to early autumn. Water more sparingly during the winter.
Temperature Normal room temperatures are suitable, with a winter minimum of 7°C (45°F).
Humidity The plumbago can tolerate dry air, but prefers higher humidity in warm temperatures.
Extra point Flowers are produced only on young (the new season's) growth so prune old stems drastically each spring and train the new growth.

Decorating tip
Train the new season's growth up thin canes or trellis-work for a stunning display of pale blue flowers.

158

Podocarpus macrophyllus

BUDDHIST PINE

This conifer is prized for its closely packed leaves (actually needles) that grow on elegantly drooping stems. It grows relatively slowly and a plant will change little over several years.

Light Provide bright filtered light throughout the year.
Water Water moderately and feed with a standard liquid fertilizer once every two weeks during the active growth period. Water sparingly during the winter.
Temperature Normal room temperatures are suitable, with a minimum of 10°C (50°F) in winter.
Humidity The podocarpus prefers increased humidity. Mist-spray the plant regularly if it is being grown in a warm room.

Decorating tip
This plant has an oriental feel to it that can be accentuated by growing it in a Chinese-style pot. Stand a pair of pots, with a podocarpus in each, sentinel-like on either side of patio doors.

159

Polypodium aureum

HARE'S FOOT FERN

The fronds of this fern gently arch on long stalks from a thick, creeping rhizome (see page 142) that is covered in reddish scales.

Light Grow in medium light.
Water Water plentifully and feed with a standard liquid fertilizer once every two weeks during the active growth period. Water moderately during the winter.
Temperature Normal room temperatures are ideal but the plant can survive a minimum of 10°C (50°F). Some fronds will be shed at the lower temperature.
Humidity This plant prefers extra humidity. Stand the pot on moist pebbles and mist-spray the foliage.

> **Decorating tip**
> *This fern looks most attractive displayed on a shelf at eye level, where its unusual creeping rhizome, that will crawl and hang over the edge of the pot, can be clearly seen.*

160

Polyscias balfouriana 'Pennockii'

BALFOUR ARALIA

The large, crinkly leaves of this plant have pale yellowish-green markings along their veins.

Light The plant needs bright filtered light throughout most of the year and direct sunlight in the winter.
Water Water moderately throughout the year. Feed with a standard liquid fertilizer once every two weeks during the active growth period.
Temperature This plant needs continuous and steady warmth, and will not tolerate a temperature below 20°C (65°F).
Humidity A high level of humidity is needed. Stand the pot on a tray filled with moist pebbles.

> **Decorating tip**
> *Plant a young polyscias in a dish garden with spiky-leaved plants such as Chlorophytum comosum, to create interesting contrast.*

161

Primula malacoides

FAIRY PRIMROSE

This primula has an indoor life of about eight to ten weeks and is best grown as a temporary flowering house plant (see page 142). Flowers appear in tiers and may be white, pale mauve, pink or red. Flowering plants can be bought from late winter to early spring.

Light This plant needs direct sun. Winter sun will not harm it.
Water Water plentifully, never allowing the potting mixture to dry out. Feed with a standard liquid fertilizer every two weeks.
Temperature The cooler this plant is kept, the longer the flowers will last. The ideal temperature is around 10-12°C (50-55°F).
Humidity This plant prefers increased humidity if being kept in a warm room; stand the pot on a tray of moist pebbles.

> **Decorating tip**
> *Arrange several primulas of the same colour in a simple wicker basket and position this in a cool entrance porch to provide a welcoming feature to your home.*

162

Primula obconica
PRIMULA

Capable of flowering for much of the year, this primula can be bought in flower from winter through to mid-summer. The flowers may be white, mauve, or shades of pink and red. It is usually treated as a temporary house plant (see page 142) and thrown away when the flowers die.

Light Grow in bright filtered light.
Water Water a primula plentifully and feed once every two weeks with a standard liquid fertilizer whilst flowering continues.
Temperature The cooler this plant is kept, the longer its flowers will last. An ideal temperature is about 12-18°C (55-65°F).
Humidity A primula needs high humidity. Stand the pot on a tray of moist pebbles.
Extra point The fine hairs that grow on the leaves of this plant can cause a skin rash if handled.

Decorating tip

Display several primulas together in a group for a striking and long-lasting tabletop arrangement.

163

Pteris cretica
CRETAN BRAKE

The cretan brake is a small fern with fronds divided into as many as nine ribbon-like sections. Many interesting varieties exist, some with frilled or crested frond segments and some with white stripes. The plant forms clumps from a rhizome running just under the surface of the mixture.

Light Grow in medium light.
Water Water plentifully and feed with half-strength standard liquid fertilizer once a month during the active growth period. Water moderately if the temperature falls below 15°C (60°F) in winter.
Temperature Normal room temperatures are suitable, with a winter minimum of 12°C (55°F).
Humidity This plant requires high humidity at all times. Stand the pot on a tray of moist pebbles and mist-spray the plant frequently.

Decorating tip

Grow the cretan brake in a group of other ferns and plants that prefer relatively low light levels in a shady window or dull corner of a room.

164

Punica granatum 'Nana'

DWARF POMEGRANATE

The dwarf pomegranate can flower and fruit when it is no more than 30 cm (1 ft) tall. Its orangey-red flowers appear through spring and summer.

Light Grow in direct sunlight.
Water Water plentifully and feed once every two weeks with a standard liquid fertilizer during the active growth period. Water very sparingly during the rest period.
Temperature Normal room temperatures are suitable during the active growth period but the plant needs a winter rest at a temperature of around 12°C (55°F).
Humidity Moderate humidity is needed during the active growth period; stand the pot on moist pebbles.

Decorating tip
Grow the dwarf pomegranate on a kitchen window-sill in bright sunlight, where its bell-shaped flowers and weighty fruit will be seen in close-up.

165

Rebutia minuscula

RED CROWN CACTUS

This globe-shaped cactus quickly develops many clumps and in late spring it half-covers itself with 4 cm (1½ in) long, crimson-red flowers.

Light Grow in direct sunlight throughout the year.
Water Water moderately and feed once every two weeks with a tomato-type liquid fertilizer (see page 133) from spring to autumn. Water sparingly during the winter.
Temperature Normal room temperatures are suitable for most of the year, but a cool winter rest period at around 7°C (45°F) is best for profuse flowering.
Humidity A low level of humidity is acceptable for this cactus.

Decorating tip
Grow a rebutia in a simple, shallow terracotta pan or half-pot on a sunny window-sill. The cactus will quickly cover the surface of the potting mixture and there will be a mass of spectacular flowers.

166

Rhapis excelsa

LADY PALM

This fan-leaf palm has wide frond segments. A mature plant can grow to 150 cm (5 ft) tall.

Light Grow in bright filtered light throughout the year.
Water Water moderately and feed once a month with a standard liquid fertilizer during the active growth period. Water sparingly during the winter rest period.
Temperature Normal room temperatures are suitable, but this plant will also do well in temperatures as low as 10°C (50°F).
Humidity This plant benefits from increased humidity in a warm room. Stand the pot on a tray of moist pebbles. Mist-spray the plant occasionally to clear the fronds of dust.

Decorating tip
With its oriental feel, this palm looks quite distinctive displayed in a cool, plain interior, such as a well-lit bathroom.

167

Rhipsalidopsis gaertneri

EASTER CACTUS

The Easter cactus can flower at any time in the spring. The scarlet, bell-shaped flowers appear mainly on the tips of the stem segments (there are no proper leaves) and the flowering period can last five to six weeks. The plant is upright-growing at first but as the stems lengthen, they tend to arch over and begin to trail. This plant can grow up to 30 cm (1 ft) high.

Light Grow in medium light throughout the year. This plant will benefit from standing outside in a shady spot during the summer.
Water Water plentifully during the active growth period and moderately during the winter, but never allow the pot to stand in water. As the first tiny flowerbuds are seen in early spring, start to feed once every two weeks with a tomato-type liquid fertilizer (see page 133). This will encourage more profuse flowering. Reduce watering and stop feeding the plant after the flowering stops, to encourage it to take a brief rest period. Resume watering about a month later and restart feeding, but this time at monthly intervals.
Temperature Keep a rhipsalidopsis in a warm temperature all year; it cannot tolerate a winter temperature below 10°C (50°F).
Humidity This plant needs high humidity; mist-spray it frequently and stand the pot on a large tray filled with moist pebbles.

Decorating tip
Display this plant in a hanging basket for a lovely splash of spring colour. Plant two or three young plants together in a 15-20 cm (6-8 in) basket and hang it to one side of a well-lit window.

168

Rhipsalidopsis rosea

This rhipsalidopsis has smaller stem segments than the Easter cactus. The segments are blue-green and the flowers are a soft rose-pink. It flowers profusely in spring.

Light Grow in medium light, avoiding hot summer sun.
Water Water plentifully during the active growth period and moderately during the winter. Follow the suggested feeding and rest period treatment given for *Rhipsalidopsis gaertneri* (see left).
Temperature This plant enjoys a warm temperature, with a winter minimum of 10°C (50°F).
Humidity The rhipsalidopsis likes a high level of humidity. Mist-spray the foliage frequently and stand the pot on a tray of moist pebbles.

Decorating tip
This plant will make a decorative feature in a sunless window where few other plants will thrive. Display it in a simple white container for the best effect.

169

Rhododendron simsii

AZALEA

The azalea is a small woody-stemmed shrub that can be brought into bloom from late autumn through to mid-spring. It is generally regarded as a temporary house plant (see page 142), to be discarded when the flowers die. Its flowers are usually large and rather floppy and coloured white, magenta, or any shade of pink or red. Some flowers have ruffled petal edges and some have petal edging in another shade or colour.

Light Grow this plant in bright filtered light at all times.
Water Water an azalea plentifully and feed with a standard liquid fertilizer once every two weeks whilst the plant is flowering.

Temperature This plant prefers a cool temperature at around 12°C (55°F) for its flowers to last.
Humidity The azalea prefers high humidity. Stand the pot on a tray filled with moist pebbles and mist-spray the foliage frequently (being careful not to wet the flowers).

Decorating tip
The beautiful trumpet-shaped flowers of the azalea are best appreciated at night by displaying the plant under a table lamp. This position also assists the plant to open up its flowerbuds. Make sure the plant receives enough light during the day.

170

Rhoeo spathacea 'Variegata'

MOSES IN THE CRADLE

The common name of this plant comes from the way that the white flowers are cradled in long-lasting, cup-like, purple bracts (see page 142) in the axils of the leaves. The leaves of this plant have decorative yellow stripes running down their length; these may be tinged pink in bright light. Offsets are produced around the base.

Light Grow in bright filtered light, avoiding hot summer sun.
Water Water plentifully and feed once every two weeks with a standard liquid fertilizer during the active growth period. Water sparingly during the winter.
Temperature This plant likes warmth and must have a winter minimum of 15°C (60°F).
Humidity A high level of humidity is necessary; stand the pot on a tray filled with moist pebbles and mist-spray the plant on warm days.

Decorating tip
This plant is best viewed in isolation. Raise it up a little on a glass shelf fitted into a bright window, so the deep purplish-red undersides of the leaves can be seen.

171

Saintpaulia hybrids

AFRICAN VIOLET

The African violet is deservedly one of the most popular of all house plants grown. It is readily available in many sizes, with different growth habits and with flowers of varying shapes, forms and colours.

Light This plant requires bright filtered light from spring to autumn, and direct sunlight in the winter.

Water Water moderately and feed the plant once every two weeks during the active growth period with a liquid fertilizer specially prepared for African violets. Some growers add a quarter of the recommended strength of liquid fertilizer to every watering. As plants are normally grown in peat-based potting mixtures which have little food content, this regular method of feeding is useful.

Temperature This plant does best in temperatures of between 17°-22°C (65°-75°F) but will pass through a winter rest period successfully at 12°C (55°F).

Humidity High humidity is essential for the African violet to thrive. Stand the pot on a saucer filled with moist pebbles to increase the humidity level.

Decorating tip
Mass several African violets together in a shallow basket for a colourful tabletop decoration. Flowers of the same colour will make a rich, bold statement, while the addition of a white African violet will provide a cooling effect.

METHODS OF WATERING

Extra point There are two methods of watering a saintpaulia. Either water it from above, or stand the pot in a shallow dish filled with water, and allow the mixture to take up its water needs. Both ways can be successful but be careful not to wet the leaves, and never allow the plants to get too wet or rot will set in.

172

Sansevieria trifasciata 'Laurentii'

MOTHER-IN-LAW TONGUE

The yellow-margined fleshy leaves of this plant are very attractive and can grow to 1 m (3 ft) tall.

Light Grow this plant in direct sunlight or bright filtered light.

Water Water moderately and feed with a standard liquid fertilizer once every two weeks during the active growth period. Water sparingly during the winter.
Temperature Normal room temperatures are suitable, with a winter minimum of 12°C (55°F).
Humidity This plant is tolerant of dry air and needs no extra humidity.

Decorating tip
Sansevierias can add height and stark contrast to a group of plants, particularly when associated with plants that have plain green, feathery leaves, such as Blechnum gibbum, Asplenium bulbiferum *or* Nephrolepis exaltata.

173

Saxifraga stolonifera

MOTHER-OF-THOUSANDS

The popular name of this plant comes from the many "offspring" that hang on red stolons (see page 142) from the parent plant. The marbled leaves have red undersides. There is also a variegated form, *S.s.* 'Tricolor'.

Light This plant needs bright filtered light. The variegated form needs direct sunlight.
Water Water plentifully and feed with a standard liquid fertilizer once every two weeks during the active growth period. Water moderately during winter.
Temperature This plant needs a minimum of 10°C (50°F).
Humidity This saxifraga prefers increased humidity.

Decorating tip
Grow this plant in a hanging basket in a brightly-lit window, where the marbled leaves can be shown to their full advantage.

174

Schlumbergera truncata

CLAW CACTUS

The claw cactus has stem segments with notched prickly-looking edges and bright rose-pink flowers. The flowers appear in late autumn and early winter.

Light Grow in medium light for most of the year but move to bright filtered light during the winter. Do not change the level of light whilst the plant is in bud or bloom or the buds and flowers might fall off.
Water Water plentifully for most of the year. Encourage a plant to take a short rest immediately after flowering, by reducing the amount of watering. Water only moderately during the winter. Feed once a month from early spring to autumn, with a tomato-type liquid fertilizer (see page 133).

Temperature Normal room temperatures are suitable.
Humidity A high level of humidity is essential. Stand the pot on a tray of moist pebbles and mist-spray the foliage frequently.
Extra point A plant can stand outside in a sheltered and shady part of the garden for the summer. This will harden up the stem sections and encourage generous flowering.

Decorating tip
Display a schlumbergera in a small hanging basket. Plant several small rooted cuttings in one basket and allow the stems to cascade over the basket edge and you will be rewarded in late autumn and early winter with many striking flowers.

175

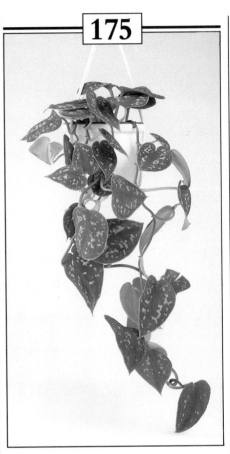

Scindapsus pictus 'Argyraeus'

SILVER VINE

The leaves of silver vine are liberally spotted with silver. The plant can be trained to climb or left to trail.

Light Grow in bright filtered light.
Water Water moderately and feed every two weeks with a standard liquid fertilizer from spring to autumn. Water sparingly in winter.
Temperature This plant likes warmth but needs a winter rest at around 15°C (60°F).
Humidity The silver vine needs high humidity to grow well.

Decorating tip
Plant two or three small plants in one pot and train them up a moss-covered pole for a striking column of silvery green.

176

Sedum lineare 'Variegata'

This very simple sedum adds a light frothy look to a mixed planting and is a very easy house plant to grow. It is fast-growing but never gets out of hand. Bright yellow flowers are produced in late spring or summer.

Light Grow this sedum in direct sunlight for the best leaf colouring.
Water Water moderately during spring, summer and autumn and sparingly in winter. It is not necessary to feed this sedum.

Temperature Grow this plant in a warm room for most of the year but encourage it to take a winter rest at around 10°C (50°F).
Humidity The sedum prefers dry air and does not need extra humidity.

Decorating tip
Tuck a few cuttings of sedum into a succulent garden where they will contrast with solid-leaved plants, such as Crassula ovata and Echeveria derenbergii.

177

Sedum morganianum

DONKEY'S TAIL

This sedum produces trailing stems up to 1 m (3 ft) long that are closely covered with fleshy, green leaves.

Light Grow in direct sunlight.
Water Water moderately during the active growth period and very sparingly during the winter rest period. A plant grown in a soil-based potting mixture (see page 134) does not need feeding.
Temperature Normal room temperatures are suitable, with a winter rest at around 10°C (50°F).
Humidity A low humidity level is acceptable for this sedum.

Decorating tip
The donkey's tail is only really safe and displayed to its best advantage when grown in a small hanging basket. Grow it in a sunny window where it will look most delightful.

178

Senecio articulatus

CANDLE PLANT

This succulent plant develops a few fleshy leaves in the autumn and winter that last a few weeks; then the pencil-like bodies of the plant stand leafless, one section on top of another.

Light Grow in direct sunlight.
Water Water moderately all year. No feeding is necessary.
Temperature Normal room temperatures are suitable.
Humidity This plant is tolerant of dry air and needs no extra humidity.

Decorating tip
This is a perfect plant for a child's room. Each section of stem is similar to a link in a chain of sausages – just what children love! Stand it on a low table or shelf.

179

Senecio macroglossus 'Variegatum'

VARIEGATED WAX VINE

This plant looks so much like an ivy that people mistake it for one. (Another common name is Cape ivy.) Its leaves are, however, fleshy and succulent, unlike ivy leaves that are leathery and pliable. In the variegated form some of the leaves are creamy yellow virtually all over; its stems and leaf stalks are purple.

Light Grow in direct sunlight throughout the year.
Water Water moderately and feed once every two weeks with a standard liquid fertilizer from early spring to mid-autumn. Water sparingly in the winter rest period.
Temperature Grow the variegated wax vine in a warm room for most of the year but move it to a cooler temperature, at around 10-12°C (50-55°F) for the winter rest period.
Humidity This plant is undemanding in this respect and does not require extra humidity.
Extra points This plant's leaves are easily damaged, so handle the plant with care. When buying a variegated wax vine, see that you get an undamaged plant. Greenfly (aphids) are often found on the soft growing tips of this plant, so keep a careful check for any single insects and thereby avoid an attack.

Decorating tip
Train the variegated wax vine around a short trellis pushed into the potting mixture for a lovely decorative display. Allow the odd strand or two to stray from the support to soften the effect.

180

Senecio rowleyanus

STRING OF BEADS

This senecio's spherical leaves appear to be strung on thin stems. Its whitish flowers appear in early winter.

Light Grow in direct sunlight.
Water Water moderately and feed once a month with a standard liquid fertilizer during the active growth period. Water sparingly in winter.
Temperature Keep in a warm room but ensure a cool winter rest period at around 7-12°C (45-55°F).
Humidity The string of beads is able to withstand dry air.

Decorating tip
Plant several young plants in a small hanging basket in a bright window and allow the stems to hang in long trails.

181

Setcreasea pallida 'Purple Heart'

PURPLE HEART

This large-leaved tradescantia relative has 8-15 cm (3-6 in) long, violet-purple leaves and strong pink flowers.

Light Grow in direct sunlight throughout the year for this plant to take on its strongest leaf colour.
Water Water moderately through the active growth period but always allow the potting mixture to dry out considerably between applications. Water sparingly in winter. When the plant is well established, feed it once a month with a standard liquid fertilizer. Stop feeding during the winter rest period.
Temperature This plant is tolerant of a wide range of temperatures, but requires a winter minimum temperature of 7-12°C (45-55°F).
Humidity The purple heart is unaffected by dry air and does not require extra humidity.
Extra point As this plant grows older, it becomes rather leggy. It is therefore best to replace the plant annually by taking cuttings.

Decorating tip
Plant a purple heart in a basket with a green-leaved tradescantia, such as Tradescantia sillamontana *for strong leaf contrast and an attractive display.*

182

Sinningia cardinalis

CARDINAL FLOWER

The cardinal flower produces fleshy, hairy leaves and, in late summer, tube-shaped scarlet flowers.

Light Grow in bright filtered light.
Water Water sparingly in spring, then plentifully during the flowering period. When the flowering stops, feed once every two weeks with half-strength tomato-type liquid fertilizer (see page 133) until the top growth dies down. Keep the plant virtually dry during the rest period.
Temperature This plant likes warmth but 10-12°C (50-55°F) is suitable for the rest period.
Humidity This plant benefits from humidity during the warmer months. Stand the pot on moist pebbles.

Decorating tip
Display two or three cardinal flowers together in a small terracotta trough in a sunny window.

183

Sinningia pusilla hybrids

MINIATURE PUSILLA HYBRIDS

In recent years the miniature sinningia, *S. pusilla*, and the many hybrids raised from it and other species, have become very popular. The species is no more than 13 mm ($\frac{1}{2}$ in) tall with violet or lavender tube-shaped flowers. The hybrids may be a little bigger but all are still very small and in the right conditions they flower virtually continuously. Small pea-sized tubers are developed and the plant seeds freely. Among the many hybrids to look out for are *S.* 'Bright Eyes', with light and dark purple flowers, *S.* 'Dollbaby', with bluish-lilac and white flowers and *S.* 'Pink Petite' with pink flowers.

Light Grow the miniature sinningia in bright filtered light, avoiding direct sunlight, throughout the year.
Water Water moderately while growth persists but more sparingly during the winter. Feed an actively growing plant with a *very* weak tomato-type liquid fertilizer (see page 133) once every two weeks.
Temperature Keep this plant in a warm room.
Humidity Herein lies the secret of success. A high level of humidity is essential; stand the pot on a tray of moist pebbles, ideally in a glazed case (see below), but do not mist-spray the plant as this can spoil the flowers and leaves.

A single pusilla hybrid in a brandy glass

Decorating tip
Grow several miniature sinningias in individual 5-6 cm (2-2$\frac{1}{2}$ in) pots and sit them in a thin layer of moist peat, sphagnum moss or small pebbles in a small decorative terrarium, fish tank, or glass bowl. Keep the base material constantly moist.

184

Smithiantha zebrina hybrids

TEMPLE BELLS

The smithiantha is grown for its attractive foliage and its late autumn and winter flower spikes. It has a long dormant rest period when the foliage dies and on this account it is often kept as a temporary plant (see page 142).

Light Grow in medium light for most of the year but move to bright filtered light for the flowering period.
Water Water moderately whilst the plant is in flower. Gradually reduce watering after flowering and keep the plant totally dry for the rest period. No feeding is necessary.
Temperature The smithiantha requires constant warmth.
Humidity This plant needs high humidity; stand the pot on a tray of moist pebbles, but do not mist-spray the plant as this can mark the foliage.

Decorating tip
Stand this plant on a low table in an entrance hall. It looks particularly striking viewed from above when its bright flowers are set against the velvety leaves.

185

Solanum capsicastrum

JERUSALEM CHERRY

The Jerusalem cherry can be bought in autumn and winter. It is usually treated as a temporary house plant (see page 142) and discarded when the berries wither and die.

Light Grow in direct sunlight.
Water Water plentifully and feed once every two weeks with a standard liquid fertilizer.
Temperature The Jerusalem cherry prefers a cool room temperature at around 15°C (60°F).
Humidity This plant needs high humidity. Stand the pot on moist pebbles and mist-spray frequently.
Extra point The berries are poisonous so keep the plant away from young children who may be attracted by their bright colours.

Decorating tip
The striking contrast between the small, dark green leaves and the shiny, orange-red berries can add a festive note to a Christmas display. Arrange several small plants in a brass bowl or small copper trough for a lovely splash of colour.

186

Sparmannia africana

INDOOR LIME

The indoor lime has large, apple-green leaves and small, white flowers with striking yellow stamens. The flowering period is very prolonged, from winter to early summer.

Light Grow in bright filtered light.
Water Water a young indoor lime moderately. When it has filled its pot with roots, water plentifully. Feed once every two weeks with a standard liquid fertilizer all year.
Temperature Normal room temperatures are suitable.
Humidity This plant benefits from increased humidity when grown in a warm room. Stand the pot on a tray filled with moist pebbles.

Decorating tip

Stand this large plant in a well-lit window where the sunlight will enhance its soft green leaves, and display the flower clusters to their best advantage.

187

Spathiphyllum hybrids

WHITE SAILS

The dark green leaves of this plant provide a perfect foil for the pure white spathes (see page 142) that give this plant its common name.

Light Grow in medium light.
Water Water moderately and feed once every two weeks with a standard liquid fertilizer during the period from early spring to mid-autumn. Water sparingly for the winter rest period.
Temperature This spathiphyllum enjoys warmth, with a winter minimum of 12°C (55°F).
Humidity This plant needs high humidity. Stand the pot on moist pebbles and mist-spray regularly. Do not wet the spathes as this can cause rot.

Decorating tip

This plant has a lovely cool feel and is best displayed on its own; grow it in a simple, modern interior away from the distracting foliage or flowers of other plants.

188

Stenotaphrum secundatum 'Variegatum'

VARIEGATED BUFFALO GRASS

This decorative grass has blunt leaf edges and a creeping habit of growth. It can grow to 60 cm (2 ft) long.

Light Grow in very bright light, including some direct sunlight, or the leaves will lose their cream striping.
Water This is a thirsty plant and should be watered plentifully during the active growth period, but more sparingly during the winter rest period. Feed once a month with a standard liquid fertilizer during the active growth period only.
Temperature This plant will grow in normal room temperatures, with a winter minimum of 12°C (55°F).
Humidity This plant needs high humidity. Stand the pot on a tray of moist pebbles and mist-spray the foliage frequently.

Decorating tip
The variegated buffalo grass is best displayed in a hanging basket placed in a sunny window where it will create a light, frothy effect.

189

Streptocarpus hybrids

CAPE PRIMROSE

The blue-flowered hybrid *S.* 'Constant Nymph' and the John Innes hybrids make very good house plants. The latter hybrids have large funnel-shaped flowers in shades of pink, red, blue and mauve, and most have darker veining in their centres. The leaves are coarse and primrose-like but those of the recommended hybrids are not too big, a common fault with many other varieties.

Light Grow in bright filtered light for most of the year but if a plant continues to flower in autumn and winter, move it into direct sunlight to prolong the flowering.
Water Water moderately and feed once every two weeks with a tomato-type liquid fertilizer (see page 133) from spring to autumn. Encourage the plant to have a rest period by reducing watering in winter.
Temperature Normal room temperatures are suitable, but the plant prefers a winter rest at around 12°C (55°F).
Humidity This plant needs high humidity at all times. Stand the pot on a tray of moist pebbles.
Extra point The streptocarpus is shallow-rooting and is best grown in a half-pot. Repot each spring.

Decorating tip
The vibrant colours of the modern varieties of streptocarpus can be best displayed with green foliage plants in a trough or a wicker basket on a low table.

SUCCULENTS & CACTI

Succulent plants are those that have adapted to growing in a dry, inhospitable area. Some produce a few sparse leaves, others produce many very fleshy leaves, whilst some have none at all. Many succulents are able to store water in their leaves and stems as an insurance against periods of drought. Another characteristic of many succulents is the dense covering of hair, wool, spines or prickles, which were developed to baffle the drying effects of sun or wind, or both. Cacti are a family of plants, all of which are succulents. They can be distinguished by their areoles (see page 142) which often bear spines and from which flowers are produced.

Cultivation

Succulents usually have extensive root systems as they are used to searching for water. They must have a well-drained potting mixture. All succulents prefer to have a thorough watering and then be allowed to dry out before being watered again. During the winter, succulents should have a drier rest period. Most succulents like to have as much light as possible; they benefit from a short spell in a sheltered but sunny part of the garden during summer and early autumn. This strengthens the leaves and stems and heightens the colour.

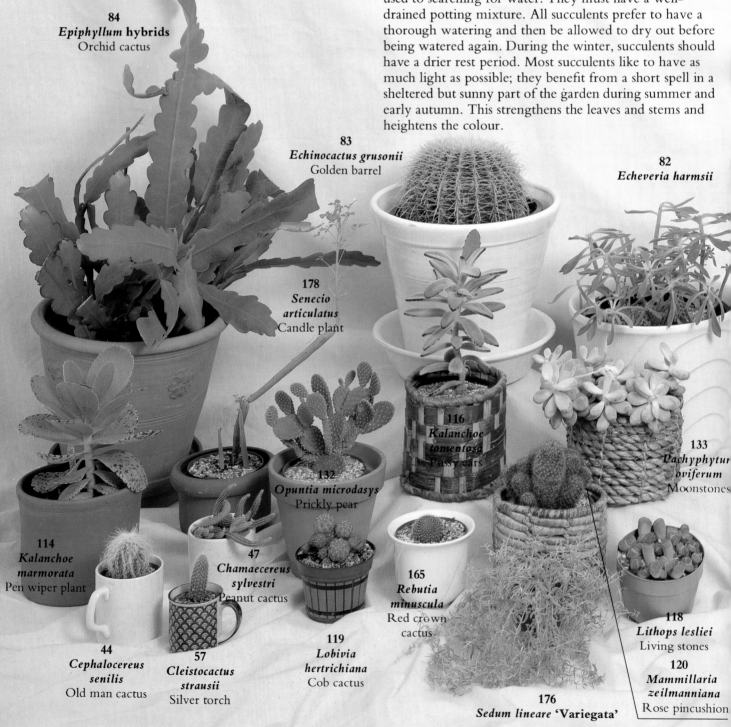

84
Epiphyllum **hybrids**
Orchid cactus

83
Echinocactus grusonii
Golden barrel

82
Echeveria harmsii

178
Senecio articulatus
Candle plant

116
Kalanchoe tomentosa
Pussy ears

133
Pachyphytum oviferum
Moonstones

114
Kalanchoe marmorata
Pen wiper plant

132
Opuntia microdasys
Prickly pear

47
Chamaecereus sylvestri
Peanut cactus

165
Rebutia minuscula
Red crown cactus

118
Lithops lesliei
Living stones

44
Cephalocereus senilis
Old man cactus

57
Cleistocactus strausii
Silver torch

119
Lobivia hertrichiana
Cob cactus

120
Mammillaria zeilmanniana
Rose pincushion

176
Sedum lineare 'Variegata'

63
Cotyledon undulata
Silver crown

81
Echeveria derenbergii
Painted lady

4
Aeonium arboreum

113
Kalanchoe blossfeldiana
hybrids
Flaming Katy

115
Kalanchoe
'Tessa'

177
Sedum morganianum
Donkey's tail

13
Aporocactus flagelliformis
Rat's tail cactus

8
Aloe barbadensis
Medicine plant

46
Ceropegia woodii
Rosary vine

174
Schlumbergera truncata
Claw cactus

45
Cereus peruvianus
Peruvian apple cactus

66
Crassula ovata
Jade plant

7
Aloe aristata
Lace aloe

65
Crassula lycopodioides
Watch-chain crassula

64
Crassula falcata
Sickle plant

180
Senecio rowleyanus
String of beads

100
Haworthia margaritifera
Pearl plant

167
Rhipsalidopsis gaertneri
Easter cactus

168
Rhipsalidopsis rosea

190

Syngonium podophyllum

ARROWHEAD PLANT

The arrowhead plant is a fast-growing climber that can easily grow to 160-200 cm (5-6 ft) tall.

Light Grow in bright filtered light, avoiding hot summer sun.
Water Water moderately and feed once every two weeks with a standard liquid fertilizer from early spring to late autumn. Water sparingly during the winter to encourage the plant to have a rest period.
Temperature Normal room temperatures are suitable, with a minimum of 12°C (55°F).
Humidity This tropical climber requires high humidity; stand the pot on a tray of moist pebbles and mist-spray the plant on warm days.

Decorating tip
Train a syngonium up a moss-covered pole and keep it moist at all times. The plant will respond to the extra rooting space and added humidity by producing sturdy growth, large leaves and strongly contrasting leaf markings.

191

Thunbergia alata

BLACK-EYED SUSAN

The flowers of this fast-growing climber may be orange, creamy-yellow or, more rarely, white. Most blooms have a distinctive chocolate-coloured "eye". The flowering period lasts from spring to autumn. Black-eyed Susan is best treated as a temporary plant (see page 142) and discarded when it stops flowering.

Light Grow in direct sunlight.
Water Water a well-developed plant plentifully and feed once every two weeks with a standard liquid fertilizer.
Temperature Normal room temperatures are suitable.
Humidity Black-eyed Susan benefits from increased humidity in a warm room. Stand the pot on a large tray filled with moist pebbles.

Decorating tip
Allow a plant to clamber and twine up and over a trellis made of thin bamboo canes. Some tying in of the stems may be necessary. Remove the flowers as they die, as this extends the flowering period.

192

Tillandsia cyanea

BLUE-FLOWERED TORCH

The very grass-like but leathery leaves of this rosette-shaped plant are in strong contrast to the fleshy, pink flower-head. This is made up of overlapping bracts with large, three-petalled purple-blue flowers peeping through. The bracts change colour from green to rose red at flowering time. The actual flowers do not last long, but the bracts remain decorative for several weeks. Like most bromeliads the rosette of leaves dies after flowering. Offsets form around the base of the plant and, when they are well developed, they can be removed to propagate the plant.

Light Grow in direct sunlight.

Water Water sparingly at all times. This tillandsia is not an "atmospheric airplant" as is *T. ionantha* (see page 116) but it needs very little water at any time. Feed with half-strength standard liquid fertilizer once a month in spring and summer.

Temperature Grow the tillandsia in a warm room and never allow the temperature to fall below 12°C (55°F).

Humidity This plant needs high humidity. Stand the pot on a tray of moist pebbles and mist-spray frequently. This is how the tillandsia takes in most of its water supply.

Extra point The roots of this tillandsia are very sparse and a 5-cm (4-in) pot is big enough for a flowering-sized plant.

CUTTING A TILLANDSIA OFFSET

1 *Carefully remove the plant from its pot. Cut the offset as close as possible to the main stem.*

2 *Pot the detached offset in a separate pot of rooting mixture, at the same depth as it was before.*

Decorating tip
This plant is best seen in close-up when it flowers. Grow it on a brightly lit window-sill for most of the year, and then move it to a low table, desktop or other surface when the flower-head appears, where you will be able to appreciate the decorative, rose-red bracts.

193

Tillandsia ionantha

This tillandsia is one of the most decorative of the "airplants" or "atmospheric" tillandsias. It grows into a tufted silvery rosette up to 10 cm (4 in) tall and flushes a vivid red when it is about to flower.

Light Grow in bright filtered light throughout the year.
Water Airplants do not need watering in the usual way. Instead they need mist-spraying (with clean rainwater if possible). Allow the grey or silvery scales to dry out between sprayings. Add a quarter-strength standard liquid fertilizer to the spray once a month in spring and summer.
Temperature Normal room temperatures are suitable.
Humidity This plant enjoys high humidity. Stand it on a tray of moist pebbles and mist-spray frequently.

Decorating tip

Fix a few tillandsias to an attractive piece of driftwood and display it at the end of the bath, or suspend it from the bathroom ceiling and enjoy it as a living mobile.

194

Tolmiea menziesii

PIGGYBACK PLANT

This rather sprawling plant produces small plantlets on the top of most of its mature leaves, weighing down the leaves as they develop.

Light Grow in bright filtered light.
Water Water moderately and feed once every two weeks with a standard liquid fertilizer during the active growth period. Water sparingly in the winter months.
Temperature This plant is tolerant of a wide range of temperatures, with a winter minimum of 10°C (50°F).
Humidity High humidity is not important, but mist-spray the plant frequently in a warm room to deter red spider mites which are liable to attack this plant.

Decorating tip

Plant two or three young tolmieas in a plain pot near to a window, but out of direct sunlight. As the plants grow, they will be weighed down by the new plantlets and will droop and hang attractively over the sides of the container.

195

Tradescantia blossfeldiana 'Variegata'

This tradescantia produces large trusses of pink and white flowers in late spring and early summer.

Light Grow in bright filtered light.
Water Water plentifully and feed once every two weeks with a standard liquid fertilizer from early spring through to mid-autumn. Water more sparingly during the winter.
Temperature Normal room temperatures are suitable, with a winter minimum of 10°C (50°F).
Humidity This plant needs high humidity. Stand the pot on moist pebbles and mist-spray on warm days.

Decorating tip
Few other plants can give such a striking display as this plant grown in a hanging basket. Plant three or four young plants in spring in a basket and by late summer you will have a glorious display.

196

Tradescantia fluminensis 'Variegata'

WANDERING JEW

The popular wandering Jew develops thin, almost transparent leaves, broadly striped with white, that can flush purple in bright light.

Light Grow in direct sunlight.
Water Water plentifully and feed once every two weeks with a standard liquid fertilizer in the active growth period. Water sparingly in winter.
Temperature Provide a minimum temperature of 10°C (50°F).
Humidity This plant needs high humidity. Stand the pot on moist pebbles and mist-spray on warm days.

Decorating tip
Plant a small wandering Jew in a trough of mixed plants. Its trailing stems will spill over the edge of the container, adding colour and contrast to the arrangement.

197

Tradescantia sillamontana

WHITE VELVET

The common name of this plant comes from the long, white velvety hairs that cover its green leaves. The flowers that are occasionally produced are coloured deep mauve.

Light Grow in direct sunlight. Insufficient light leads to leggy growth and a loss of the velvety white felting.
Water Water moderately and feed once every two weeks with a standard liquid fertilizer during the active growth period. Water very sparingly in winter. Always allow some considerable drying out of the potting mixture between applications.
Temperature Normal room temperatures are suitable.
Humidity This tradescantia will thrive in quite dry air; do not mist-spray the foliage, but stand the pot on a tray filled with moist pebbles if growing the plant in a warm room.
Extra point Ensure that the potting mixture is very well drained by using a one-third portion of coarse sand or perlite, or growth will become straggly and soft.

Decorating tip
Grow this tradescantia in a hanging basket in a brightly-lit window, where it will form an attractive globe of silvery green.

198

Vriesea splendens

FLAMING SWORD

With its brown striped leaves, this striking bromeliad is attractive all year round but even more so when it sends up its flower stalk topped with a broad flower-head made up of bright red bracts. Tubular yellow flowers emerge from between the bracts. Although the actual flowers are short-lived, the flower spike remains decorative for several months. As with most bromeliads the rosette of leaves dies when the flowering period is over. Offsets are not freely produced but odd ones appear in the lower leaf axils and may be used in propagation when they are well developed.

Light Grow in very bright light, including a few hours of direct sunlight, for the strongest leaf colour and to encourage flowering. Keep it out of the hot summer sun, or the leaves may become "scorched".
Water Water plentifully and feed once every two weeks with half-strength standard liquid fertilizer from spring through to autumn. Water sparingly during the winter. Keep the centre of the rosette of leaves filled with water (use clean rainwater whenever possible), except when the flower-head is emerging, and change the water frequently.
Temperature Normal room temperatures throughout the year are suitable for this plant.
Humidity The vriesea benefits from humidity; stand the pot on a large tray filled with moist pebbles and mist-spray the plant regularly.

Decorating tip
Display the flaming sword, on its own, on a low table or other surface where it can be viewed from above. The banded leaves and striking red flower-head will then be seen to their best advantage.

199

Yucca elephantipes

YUCCA

Decorating tip
With its simple, bold shape and long, spiky leaves, the yucca can be displayed effectively against a full-length window to provide a modern sculptural silhouette.

There are two distinct types of yucca: the "stick" yucca that comprises a stout, woody trunk from which sprout two or more rosettes of dark green fleshy leaves, up to 120 cm (4 ft) long, and the "tip" yucca, which is stemless and consists of just one rosette of leaves The leafless "sticks" are usually imported from South America and are induced to develop their rosettes of leaves. The "tip" yucca is a simple rosette of leaves that has developed roots after having been cut from a stem.

Light Grow in direct sunlight throughout the year.
Water Water plentifully and feed once every two weeks with a standard liquid fertilizer during the active growth period. Water sparingly in winter.
Temperature This plant is almost frost hardy but does best when grown in temperatures above 10°C (50°F).
Humidity The yucca is unaffected by dry air, but frequent mist-spraying is advisable when the plant is grown in a warm room, as this will help to discourage red spider mites that can be a nuisance with this plant in dry air.

TYPES OF YUCCA

"Stick" yucca
(right)
"Tip" yucca
(below)

200

Zebrina pendula

WANDERING SAILOR

Wandering sailor or wandering Jew are names this plant shares with its close relative, the tradescantia. Its leaves have two broad stripes of glistening silvery-green running down their length, and deep purple undersides. Clusters of pink flowers appear in spring and summer. A variety, *Z.p.* 'Purpusii', has deep wine-red leaves.

Light For the strongest leaf colour, grow in very bright light including a few hours of direct sunlight a day, but avoid the hot summer sun. Growth becomes straggly and untidy if the light level is too low.

Water Water a zebrina moderately and feed once every two weeks with a standard liquid fertilizer from spring through to autumn. Water more sparingly during the winter rest period, giving just enough water to make the potting mixture barely moist.

Temperature The zebrina will grow in most room temperatures, with a winter minimum of 12°C (55°F). In cool conditions a zebrina will grow very slowly.

Humidity This plant benefits from increased humidity if it is being grown in a warm room. Stand the pot on a tray filled with moist pebbles.

Extra points Young zebrinas look better than older ones, so it is best to renew a plant frequently. Pinch out the growing tips regularly to encourage side shoots to develop to make the plant more bushy. To create an even bushier effect, plant several zebrinas together in one pot.

Propagating a zebrina *Take short tip cuttings 8-10 cm (3 in) long in spring. Plant four to six cuttings in an 8 cm (3 in) pot filled with an equal-parts mixture of moist peat and coarse sand. Placing several cuttings together in one pot ensures a bushy plant. Cover with a polythene bag or plastic dome for three to four weeks to conserve humidity, until the cuttings have rooted.*

Decorating tip
For an unusual and decorative display, train a zebrina up a thin bamboo trellis inserted in the potting mixture and stand this on a sunny window-sill.

DECORATING

KNOW-HOW

& PLANT CARE

Selecting Plants

Always spend some time and thought choosing a new house plant for your home; try not to buy on impulse and take only the best that you can find.

First, consider where the plant is to be displayed and therefore the growing conditions you will be providing. If you want a plant for a sunny window-ledge, look for one that will thrive in such a position; it is no use buying a plant that prefers the shade. If you want a plant for a shady position, such as an entrance hall, look for plants that will thrive in a low light level. If you are looking for a plant for the bathroom, bear in mind the high level of humidity the plant must be able to tolerate.

Size of plants
Once you have worked out which plants will do well in your house, think about their size. Although some small plants can grow quite quickly into larger ones, many others are much slower growing and change little over several years. A fast-growing plant may quickly outgrow the space allocated to it and constantly require cutting back to keep it under control, whereas a small plant can look silly and out of scale when displayed where a bigger one would be more suitable.

When and where to buy
The best time to buy new plants is from spring through to early autumn. At these times of the year, home growing conditions are closer to those of commercial growers, so the plants can settle in quickly. During the winter, there are usually adverse conditions in the home, such as central heating and dry air.

Patronize reputable garden centres and nurseries and avoid buying from draughty street markets and pavement displays outside florists in windy or cold weather. Many beautiful cyclamen plants are bought under these poor conditions each year; they appear to be in good condition when bought but, because they have been subjected to a chill or draughts, the damage quickly becomes obvious when the plant arrives home.

Good quality plants
A plant that is bought in good condition and grown well will give constant pleasure, whereas a plant that is bought in poor condition is unlikely to develop into a good specimen, however well treated.

Buy only the best. The best need not be expensive. Many of the small, popular plants that are available in early summer, such as wax begonias, busy Lizzies and black-eyed Susans are all acceptable for use indoors and are quite cheap. If you plant several together in one pot, in two or three months they will grow into an attractive medium-sized display. Small plants are also more likely to become acclimatized quickly to home growing conditions than more mature plants.

Make sure the plant you buy is healthy, vigorous-looking, with stout stems, close growth and has leaves free of damage or blemish. Avoid any plants with yellowing leaves, and those with brown leaf tips or margins. While it is possible to remove the odd offending leaf from some small plants and end up with an acceptable specimen, a torn leaf on a rubber plant *(Ficus elastica)* or philodendron will be an obvious reproach for many years.

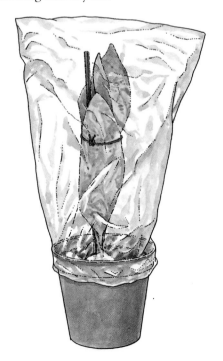

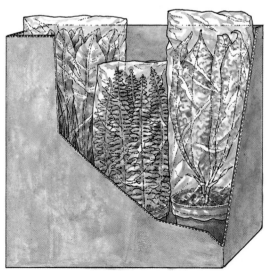

Protecting newly bought house plants
House plants are used to warm growing temperatures; any sudden change or fluctuation in temperature can damage and even kill them. Make sure when you buy a new plant, therefore, that it is well wrapped up for the journey home. A plastic sleeve (far left) will protect the plant from cold winds and draughts, while a cardboard box (left) adds a further precautionary layer of insulation.

1

2

3

What to look for

1 Check the foliage for damage or blemishes. A torn leaf on a large-leaved plant such as *Ficus elastica* is not easily disguised.

2 Check the growing tips of *Sansevieria trifasciata* for signs of damage. Once the top is broken, no further growth will occur from that point.

3 When buying a chrysanthemum, check that the buds are slightly tinged with colour. Tight green buds often fail to open indoors.

Make sure that the central growing point of a palm is intact as all future growth comes from that point. Also check that the awl-shaped tips of the leaves of the mother-in-law tongue *(Sansevieria trifasciata)* have not been damaged in any way, as once a leaf tip is damaged no further growth is possible from that leaf.

Plants bought for their flowers should be in their first flush of bloom with just a few new buds opening up. Avoid buying plants whose blooms are fully open; these can only last a few more days, whereas a plant with lots of buds still to open can continue to flower in your home for several weeks or even months. At the other extreme, however, when buying a chrysanthemum, be careful to avoid one with very tightly closed, green buds, as these can often fail to open indoors. Its buds should be slightly tinged with colour.

Inspecting a plant
Lift up your possible purchase and examine the underside of the leaves for signs of pests and the heart of the plant for slimy or rotting leaves. There should be plenty of flowerbuds on a flowering plant, and the plant should also sit firmly in its potting mixture. Avoid plants that appear to be loose in their pots.

Examine a plant carefully for any signs of pests or diseases. Sometimes the pests themselves cannot be seen but evidence of pest damage can be seen in distorted, twisted or mottled leaves and in sticky patches (see pages 138-41). If you buy a diseased plant, or one infested with pests, there is a danger of introducing the problem to the rest of your plants. Ideally you should give the plant an isolation period to ensure that it has a clean bill of health. However, this is often impractical, but a thorough examination on purchase and on your arrival home with the plant cuts out much of the risk.

HOW TO CHECK A PLANT

Checking for pests
Examine a plant carefully for pests. They usually gather around the growing tips of the stems, on flowerbuds, and on the undersides of leaves. Look out also for signs of pest damage (see pages 139-40).

Checking for stem rot
Carefully pull back the leaves to examine the heart of the plant. If there are slimy or rotting leaves visible in the centre, the stem is probably rotten and the plant is best avoided.

Displaying Plants

Where you position your house plants is largely a matter of personal taste. Some people use plants as decorating tools, much as they use lamps, sofas or rugs. They put plants where they look most effective, regardless of the growing conditions required by the actual plants. The effect is usually striking, often dramatic, but more often than not short-lived. Other people are more concerned that their house plants obtain the right amount of light, and the correct temperature and humidity, and then take very little interest in displaying them to their best advantage. The best solution is to compromise: if you combine serious regard for the growing conditions the plants need in which to thrive with some artistic flair, you will have healthy, tastefully displayed plants that fit in well with their surroundings.

Strong shapes and colours
Plants with strong leaf shapes and dramatic outlines, such as most palms, philodendrons, *Fatsia japonica,* and *Beaucarnea recurvata,* are known as "architectural" or "sculptural" plants. They act as very effective focal points in a room, immediately attracting attention, much as urns and other garden ornaments are used outside to direct the eye along a vista.

Use cool green foliage to humanize an otherwise spartan bathroom and display brightly coloured flowering plants in a dull room to cheer it up. Strong-shaped plants, like *Yucca elephantipes,* bare-stemmed dracaenas, and *Monstera deliciosa* usually look best standing against a neutral background or as silhouettes against a light source. Stark interiors can be softened with a cascade of greenery from a large *Nephrolepis exaltata* fern in a hanging basket. Fussy

backgrounds usually call for plain and simple plants with strong lines and soft colours. Colourful patterned wallpaper does not normally complement the decorative leaves of *Begonia* 'Maphil', for instance! Plants can also serve a practical purpose: create a room divider by grouping several tall, bushy plants together, or shut out an unwanted view by filling a window with greenery.

Plant groups
Just as too many decorative ornaments on a table can make it look cluttered, so too can many small plants in small pots look messy. Rather than have a row of pots running along a window-sill, why not consider grouping them together in one large container. This can be done by sinking the individual pots in moist peat, moss or expanded clay aggregate within an outer container such as a trough, decorative bowl or basket. Make sure the pots are large enough to allow each plant to grow and develop. In this way the plant arrangement will become bushier and often more attractive, as the foliage of each plant grows into that of its neighbour.

Another way of grouping plants is to take them out of their pots and plant them all directly into a larger container. This method has more permanence about it and greater care must be exercised when choosing the plants to include. It is possible to mix up the two methods of grouping plants. You could, for example, plant several foliage plants directly into a container, and then tuck in a flowering plant, still in its pot, at the front, to provide a colourful focal point. This method allows the flowering plant to be replaced as often as required without disrupting the main body of the grouping.

GROUPING PLANTS IN A CONTAINER

Cyclamen display
In this arrangement of cyclamen plants, the individual pots have been sunk into moist moss inside an unusual container.

Trailing plant arrangement *Several tradescantias and purple-flowered browallias have been planted directly into the potting mixture in a terracotta trough for an attractive display.*

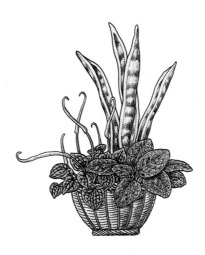

Colour and form

This arrangement presents a subtle combination of shades of green and a gently arching form. The fresh green asplenium leaves are accentuated by the darker green leaves of the aspidistra arching behind, while the small and glossy ficus leaves add a light, delicate touch at the front.

Contrasting shapes

By placing opposite shapes together, this display of plants emphasizes the differing shapes. The low, rounded form of the peperomia and fittonia plants contrast sharply with the tall, spiky leaves of the sansevieria behind, whose shape is echoed by the spindly flower spikes of the peperomia.

Feathery textures

This creative arrangement makes full use of the different feathery textures of a variety of ferns. Several adiantum, nephrolepis and asparagus ferns have been planted directly into the moist sphagnum moss of a moss pole, so that the whole column is completely covered with green foliage.

Plants with differing leaf textures often look effective growing in close association: smooth, glossy leaves can accentuate mat, ridged foliage, while delicate, feathery fern fronds can subdue larger, more solid leaves. Varying colours of foliage also add interest to a display. When mixing several plants together in such a way it is important to remember to use only plants with compatible growing needs. You cannot grow successfully a sun-loving plant with a plant that likes shade, nor a warmth-loving plant with one that prefers the cool.

An advantage of growing plants in a group is the higher level of humidity produced. All plants lose moisture into the air around them and when several plants are grown close together, as in these suggested arrangements, the air becomes charged with moisture. The plants benefit since, as one plant loses water, another takes it up.

Cactus garden

An arrangement of cacti and succulents can look attractive. You can create a cactus garden by planting up several cacti and succulents in a shallow pan or lined basket. Ideally, see that the container has drainage holes at the bottom as this greatly cuts down the danger of overwatering. Either plant the cacti directly into the potting mixture or leave the plants in their pots and sink the pots into gravel or other aggregate. For a decorative finishing touch, incorporate pieces of stone amongst the plants, or scatter a layer of gravel or white marble chippings on the surface of the potting mixture. As well as looking attractive, this also serves the useful purpose of keeping the "necks" of the cacti out of direct contact with the potting mixture.

Decorative finishes *Use stone chippings, coloured glass or shells to decorate the surface of the potting mixture.*

Training and Supporting Plants

When you first buy a young climbing plant it will probably look quite bushy and sturdy. It is only when the plant begins to grow that it will need training and supporting to prevent its stems from sprawling. Supports in the form of canes, lengths of stout wire, moss-covered poles, small trellises or lengths of cord to which plants can cling all make good solutions. Plant supports should be unobtrusive; thin canes are often sufficiently strong.

Supports should be pushed into the potting mixture whilst the plant is still very young, so it can be trained to the shape and size that you require. Many flowering climbing house plants produce more blooms when their stems are trained horizontally than when they grow vertically. Such plants are best trained around hoops of stout wire or flexible rattan cane.

Canes and trellises

The less rampant climbing plants need only a single cane or a small collection of thin canes pushed into the potting mixture to act as supports. A number of plants twine their stems around supports, some use their leaf stalks to twist around a cane and some have wiry tendrils that curl or spiral on to any suitably thin support. These plants will need no more than a support and an occasional guiding hand. Sometimes there will be an odd trailing stem, which fails to find anchorage, that can look quite effective. Climbers that have reached the limit of their supports then often arch over from the top; if space allows, let them do this. Other plants may need to be tied to their supports. Never tie any plant tightly; as the plant grows older, its stems thicken and the ties could cut into them. Use broad raffia, green-dyed twine, plant rings or wire-and-paper twists (as used for sealing plastic bags). Always fasten the tie securely to the support first, then loop the fastening loosely around the plant stem.

Strong growing plants need stronger supports. Instead of single canes, trellis-work might be more effective. To make a trellis, lash several canes securely to each other with stout twine or flexible wire, as they might eventually have to support a heavy weight of stem and foliage. The

MAKING A MOSS POLE

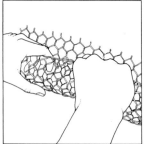

1 To form the shape of the moss pole, roll a rectangular piece of chicken wire into a tubular shape.

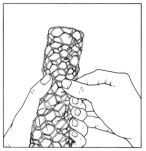

2 Secure the loose ends of the chicken wire by bending them carefully into the centre of the tube.

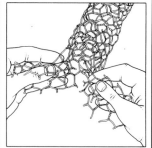

3 Cover one end of the tube with chicken wire. Cut the other end, and bend the wire back.

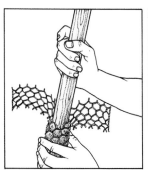

4 Holding the empty wire tube steady, fill it with sphagnum moss. Use a long wooden stick to pack it in tightly.

5 Bend the wire back to close the tube. Then stand it in the centre of a plant pot and wedge it in place with potting mixture.

6 Pot up a climbing plant in the mixture and attach its stems to the moss pole with bent wire pegs. Mist-spray regularly.

DECORATIVE SUPPORTS

Bamboo trellis

Single stakes

Cane hoop

Fan-shaped support

heavier pieces of bamboo cane that are used should ideally be drilled at appropriate fixing points, then threaded through with twists of wire, and firmly fastened. Although bamboo cane is very rigid and long lasting, it cannot be bent or twisted into different shapes. However, rattan cane can be moulded into various shapes by first soaking it in hot water or steaming it and then bending it to the required shape. For very heavy plants, large support structures standing outside the pot (for example, lattice-work attached to a wall) are a good idea, though they are not usually very practical in the home where plants and their supports need to be moved around to enable floors, walls and carpets to be cleaned.

Plants can also be trained on thin cord that is stretched between fasteners, such as small cup-hooks. Thin-foliaged plants, such as *Asparagus retrofractus* or *Ceropegia woodii* can be trained around a window in this way for a frothy display that does not block out the light. Heavier-leaved plants can be trained similarly up a wall, but the cord and supporting eyes will need to be much stronger.

Moss pole
Another method of support for some climbing plants is a moss pole. A moist moss pole will encourage aerial roots to develop on the plant (see page 142) and these will eventually grow into their support. Many philodendrons and their relatives (*Epipremnum aureum, Monstera deliciosa,* and *Scindapsus pictus*) will grow in this way, as will pileas and even ficuses, though on a smaller scale.

Pruning
All house plants need to be pruned periodically. This can be anything from what seems to be major surgery, to little more than nipping the tender growing tips out with the thumb and forefinger to encourage regular branching and a bushy appearance. Other pruning should be done with a sharp knife, scissors or secateurs. It is important that the remaining stems are not crushed.

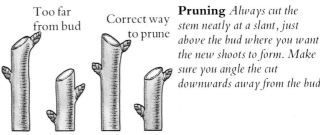

Pruning *Always cut the stem neatly at a slant, just above the bud where you want the new shoots to form. Make sure you angle the cut downwards away from the bud.*

Too far from bud · Correct way to prune · Too close to bud · Angled in wrong direction

Pinching out *To prevent some tall-growing plants from becoming too straggly and looking leggy and untidy, pinch out the growing tips regularly with thumb and forefinger. This will encourage side branches to develop, giving the plant a more bushy and compact appearance.*

Some house plants, such as *Jasminum polyanthum, Plumbago auriculata* and *Passiflora caerulea,* flower only on the stems that have grown during the current growing season; flowers do not grow on the previous year's stems. This means that most of the previous year's growth can be cut off in autumn or early spring, thereby leaving lots of room for the new flowering growth. Conversely, if you remove the older stems of *Hoya carnosa,* the plant is robbed of many of its flowering spurs which year after year make a big contribution to flower production. The rampant growing plants should normally have some of their excess stems removed annually. Thin out any tangled stems in early spring (always taking out the older stems); this will result in more air being admitted to the stem, thus allowing better ripening of younger shoots.

CUTTING BACK STRAGGLY GROWTH

1 A fast-growing plant that has been trained round a hoop can quickly outgrow its support and become straggly and untidy.

2 To cut back the plant, unravel the stems from the hoop and cut off all the old growth leaving only one or two of the youngest stems.

3 Rewind the remaining stems around the hoop, and secure them with plant rings. The hoop will soon be covered with new growth.

Choosing Containers

Gone are the days when a pot plant was simply placed in a saucer on the window-sill! Much is now made of plant display, and of matching a plant to its container. Undoubtedly the careful choice of a suitable decorative container adds to the overall effect of the arrangement.

Containers can be virtually any shape or size and made in a very wide range of materials. The most effective ones are those that completely hide the inner pot, that are in scale with the plant and of a colour and material that does not clash with the plant for attention.

Cane and wicker baskets
Large woven cane waste-paper baskets make good pot-hiders for large plants standing on the floor and have a

simple country feel. A saucer in the bottom or some stout plastic sheeting is all you need to make them waterproof. Woven cane shopping baskets in all shapes and sizes can also be used as plant containers. A basket of colourful campanulas or begonias makes for an attractive tabletop decoration, or plant up several trailing plants and then hang the basket from a hook in a window recess.

Terracotta pots
Highly decorative and chunky-looking hand-made terracotta pots add a rustic feel to a room. Plant up a variety of plants in different pots and then group them together where the contrasting leaf shapes and textures can be appreciated. Terracotta troughs are traditionally used out of doors, but they can look equally good in the house, particularly if they fit into a window recess. Remember to fit a drip tray underneath them.

New terracotta is very dry and before it is used, it needs to be soaked in water for several hours and then to be allowed to dry out slightly. If it is planted up whilst still bone dry, it will suck all the moisture out of the potting mixture, causing the mixture to shrink away from the sides of the pot and the plant to suffer.

Decorated china pots
There are any number of decorated china pots available, ranging from simple white glazed pots to highly decorated crackle-glazed "Chinese"-style pots. These often add considerably to the decorative effect of the plant. The different colours of a container can evoke different moods. Plain white glazed containers are extremely smart and can add an air of sophistication to an arrangement of plants; whereas bright cherry-red pots are more cheerful and fun to use, and can brighten up a room considerably.

Hanging baskets
The traditional open-mesh hanging baskets, made out of stout wire and lined with sphagnum moss, were used in conservatories or porches, where the attendant drip was no problem. Now, of course, you can obtain drip trays or line your hanging basket to make it waterproof, and display it in the home. Plastic pot-shaped baskets with built-in drip saucers and chains or other devices for hanging are readily available from garden centres and nurseries. But if you want to make one yourself, practically any half-circular container can be planted up and then suspended in rope or macramé hangings. A pretty finishing touch is to train the plant stems up the ropes or chains that support the basket.

Bottle gardens and terraria
Slow-growing, small plants can be displayed effectively in bottle gardens and terraria. Bottle gardens are usually

WOVEN WICKER BASKET
A simple wicker basket makes a very attractive plant container. Either leave it as it is for a simple country charm, or paint it to match the room decor for a more sophisticated feel. Here the handle of the basket has been used as a support for the climbing stems of Plumbago auriculata.

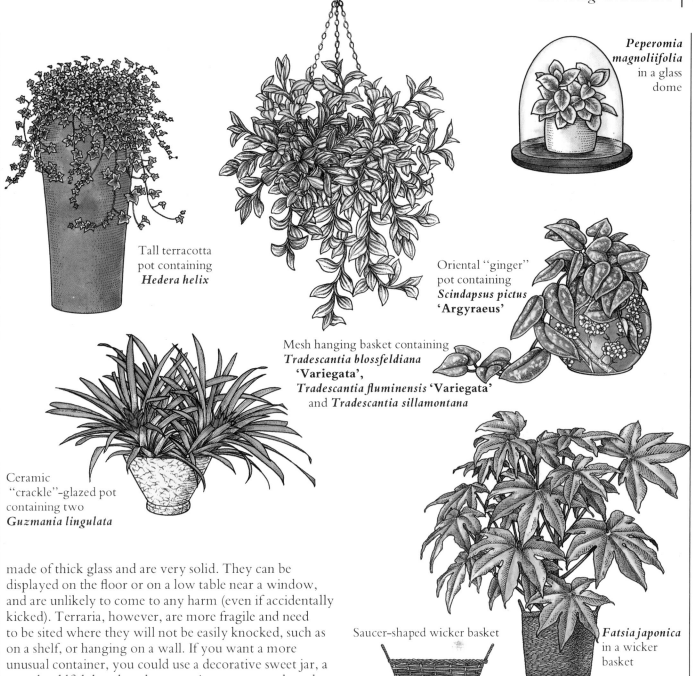

Tall terracotta
pot containing
Hedera helix

**Peperomia
magnoliifolia**
in a glass
dome

Oriental ''ginger''
pot containing
**Scindapsus pictus
'Argyraeus'**

Mesh hanging basket containing
**Tradescantia blossfeldiana
'Variegata',
Tradescantia fluminensis 'Variegata'**
and **Tradescantia sillamontana**

Ceramic
''crackle''-glazed pot
containing two
Guzmania lingulata

Saucer-shaped wicker basket

Fatsia japonica
in a wicker
basket

made of thick glass and are very solid. They can be
displayed on the floor or on a low table near a window,
and are unlikely to come to any harm (even if accidentally
kicked). Terraria, however, are more fragile and need
to be sited where they will not be easily knocked, such as
on a shelf, or hanging on a wall. If you want a more
unusual container, you could use a decorative sweet jar, a
round goldfish bowl, a glass aquarium, or even a brandy
glass. When planting up a bottle garden, make sure you
are able to reach into it so you can remove any fading leaves
and fallen flowers before rot sets in.

Quirky and unusual containers
Many household objects which are no longer used can be
given a new lease of life displaying plants. A pretty
vegetable or soup tureen can be used to hold a group of
three or four small plants and displayed on a table top.
Blue and white china foot-baths (now often seen as
collector's items) can hold up to six medium-sized plants.
Simple bread crocks, pottery jugs and straight-sided glass
containers can all look stunning when planted up. If you
keep an eye open for possible containers in antique and
junk shops, you should be able to find something slightly
quirky and out of the ordinary!

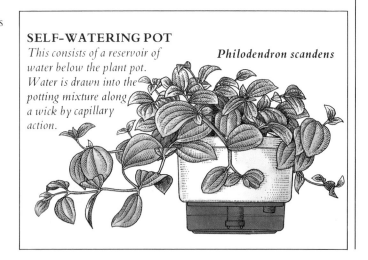

SELF-WATERING POT
*This consists of a reservoir of
water below the plant pot.
Water is drawn into the
potting mixture along
a wick by capillary
action.*

Philodendron scandens

Plant Care
LIGHT, TEMPERATURE & HUMIDITY

All plants have their likes and dislikes (some may even be very demanding) but by following the brief suggestions about light, watering, temperature and humidity given for each individual plant in the A-Z Plant Guide (pages 18-120) success can be assured. In this plant care section (pages 130-141) a more detailed account is given of the conditions plants need in order to thrive.

Light
All plants must have sufficient light to function properly and to survive. Light falling on the leaves of plants sets off a process called photosynthesis that allows the leaves to manufacture much of the food they need. When it is dark this process stops and no plant food is made.

It is very difficult for the human eye to assess the intensity of light but it should be remembered that the level of light in the home is considerably lower than that outside. It also varies in different positions in the home (see below). As well as the intensity of light, it is important to consider the light duration (day length). Some plants, such as chrysanthemums, flower only when days are relatively short (less than ten hours of daylight); others flower only after a few weeks of long days.

Temperature
Each plant has a preferred temperature range but most of the more popular house plants grow well in a wide range of temperatures. Most house plants do best in temperatures at around 15-21°C (60-70°F). Happily, these are the sort of temperatures that we feel most comfortable in. In the individual plant entries in the A-Z Plant Guide (pages 18-120) reference has been made to "normal room

Light levels in a room
This illustration shows the different levels of light in a room facing the sun. The intensity of light will vary depending on climatic conditions, the size of the window and whether there are nearby trees or tall buildings. Curtains absorb light in a room, reducing the level of light on either side of the window, and blinds also cut out a lot of light; they can be used for shading plants from direct sun. Some plants thrive only in direct sunlight; others need less light but very few plants will tolerate poor light for long.

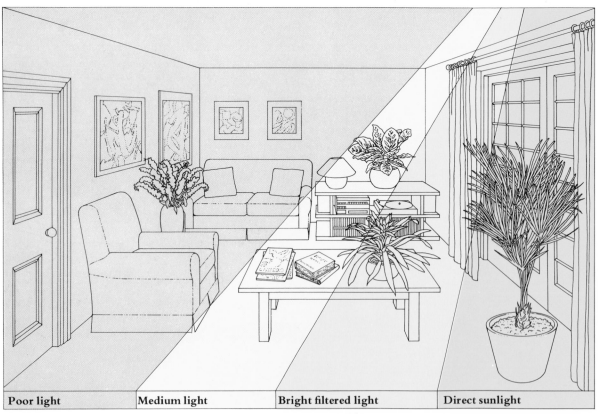

Poor light	**Medium light**	**Bright filtered light**	**Direct sunlight**
An area more than 2 m (6 ft) from the light. Plants will not thrive.	An area near a sunless window or 1.5-2 m (4-6 ft) away from a sunny window.	An area that receives direct sunlight filtered by a translucent blind or curtain.	A position that receives bright sunshine for most or at least part of the day.

temperatures" and this is taken to be that "comfortable" range. Some plants, such as the temporary flowering house plants, prefer to grow in cooler temperatures; in a warm room the flowers will not last very long. Other plants, such as cacti and a number of other succulent plants, will only flower well the following year if they are given a winter rest period at a cool temperature.

When temperatures start to rise above normal room temperatures, many plants like an increased level of humidity. Warm, dry air draws moisture out of the leaves of plants and it causes high levels of evaporation from the potting mixture. This in turn makes the plant's roots work harder at pumping moisture through its many parts.

Guard against plants being isolated at night in the chilly area between drawn curtains and the window as they might suffer from the cold. It is better to move them into the room where they will be able to enjoy the evening warmth. At the other extreme, avoid placing a house plant too near a stove or a radiator, where the temperature might be too high, or near doors and air vents, where the plants may be subject to draughts.

Humidity

Humidity is the amount of water vapour in the air. It is measured as a percentage on a scale ranging from 0 to 100 per cent. Very dry air registers at 0, whilst air that is so saturated with moisture that you can see it in the form of mist or steam could be around 100 per cent. Some plants *need* high humidity to survive. Other plants *prefer* extra humidity but they will not die if they do not receive it. A third group of plants thrives in dry air and needs no extra humidity to be provided.

TROUBLE SPOTS
Plants placed close to the trouble spots shown here will soon show signs of poor health.

Refrigerator *gives off waste heat.*

Air vent *allows cold air in.*

Radiator *heats and dries out the air.*

Open door *causes cold draughts.*

Cooker *creates intense heat.*

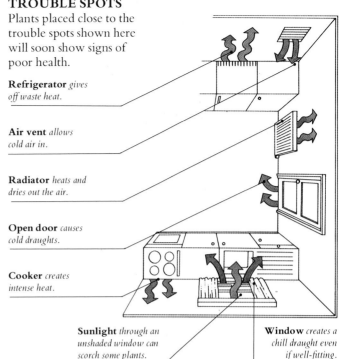

Sunlight *through an unshaded window can scorch some plants.*

Window *creates a chill draught even if well-fitting.*

An average room in a modern house has a humidity level at around 40 per cent so for most plants to thrive, that is, those *needing* and those *preferring* humidity, the humidity level must be raised. There are several methods of doing this, such as standing the plant on moist pebbles, burying the pot in moist peat and mist-spraying the foliage. Nothing, however, beats standing house plants out of doors in a gentle shower during mild weather.

INCREASING HUMIDITY

Mist-spraying *Mist-spraying a plant with a fine spray of water temporarily covers the leaves and stem with a thin film of moisture. This also discourages some pests from attacking the plant and washes off surface dust.*

Pebble-filled tray *Stand pots on a tray filled with moist pebbles. The water around the pebbles will evaporate over a few days and should then be replenished. Make sure that the pot does not stand in water or the plant's roots may become waterlogged and rot.*

Burying pots in peat *Stand one or a group of pots in a larger outer container. Fill the gap between the pots and the outer container with moist peat, so that the inner pots are buried up to their rims. Remember to water the peat occasionally to keep it moist.*

Watering

Water is essential to all plants; they need it to keep their stems and leaves turgid, upright and functioning properly, they need it to manufacture food and to bring up from the potting mixture the foods they cannot manufacture themselves. If a plant does not get enough water it will eventually die. Likewise, if it receives too *much* water, it will also die. See the individual plant articles in the A-Z Plant Guide on pages 18-120 for the recommended quantity of water to be given to each plant.

How to water
One method is to water a plant from above by pouring water on to the surface of the potting mixture and allowing the water to soak downwards. Another method is to stand the pot in a deep saucer filled with water and allow the potting mixture to take up the amount of water it needs by capillary action. Both methods have advantages and disadvantages. Watering from below avoids wetting the leaves, stems and crown of a plant (some plants are particularly liable to rot when this occurs) but if only a relatively small amount of water is given it is liable to stay in the lower levels of the potting mixture and not rise very far up. Watering from above means that the mixture is thoroughly wetted all the way through, but if a plant is watered too sparingly from above it tends not to reach down into the lower levels of the potting mixture.

A mixture of the two methods is often the best solution. Self-watering containers are available from garden centres and nurseries (see page 129). To water the plant, simply ensure the container is topped up with water.

Holiday care
The best way of seeing that your plants are looked after when you are away on holiday is to ask an enthusiastic neighbour to do your watering for you.

Failing that, move some of the hardier plants out of doors to a sheltered and shady spot, and then sink the pots in the ground (or in boxes packed with damp peat). This will keep the roots cool and moist. Plants that do not like being outdoors are best kept in bright filtered light in a humid atmosphere. There are several methods of keeping plants moist. One is to stand the plants on a draining board in the kitchen on a piece of capillary matting or absorbent felt leading to a sink partially full of water. Another method is to feed wicks into the top of the plant pot from a reservoir of water. Pots can also be placed in larger containers and the gap between them packed with saturated newspaper or very wet peat.

Feeding
Every plant needs a supply of minerals and nutrients in order to grow well. These are normally contained in a fertile garden soil. Potted plants, however, quickly use up whatever nutrients were in their potting mixture and need supplementary feeding.

Plant food is available in several forms, such as liquids, powders, granules, pills and "spikes", but the easiest and most popular method of adding nutrients to a potting mixture is by using a liquid fertilizer. This is usually added periodically to the water when a plant is watered.

OVERWATERING AND UNDERWATERING

Too much water *The leaves develop soft patches on their surfaces, they turn yellow and eventually curl up and drop. Flowers become mouldy and the roots rot. Allow the potting mixture almost to dry out before watering it again.*

Too little water *The leaves of the plant wilt and begin to curl and their edges turn brown. Flowers fade and fall very quickly. The potting mixture may shrink away from the sides of the pot. Soak the plant in a bowl of water to revive it.*

METHODS OF WATERING

To give the plant a thorough soaking, water it from above, by pouring water directly on to the potting mixture until the excess water drains through.

To avoid wetting the leaves of a plant, which might mark them with unsightly spots, water the plant from below by pouring water into the saucer.

It is essential that fertilizer is not applied to dry potting mixture as this can damage a plant's roots.

Plants only need supplementary feeding when they are growing actively, to build strong stems, large lush leaves and lots of flowers. They do not need feeding when they are resting during the winter months.

Plant food needs to contain three major ingredients for the plant to flourish: nitrogen, phosphorus and potassium. All plants need *nitrogen* to grow bigger, and to develop stout stems and healthy leaves. A shortage of nitrogen results in pale leaves and thin leggy growth. *Phosphorus* encourages healthy root growth and is needed to help form flowerbuds and to strengthen stem and leaf growth. *Potassium* gives general sturdiness, flowers and fruit of good colour and builds up bulbs for the following year. A *standard liquid fertilizer* contains equal proportions of each of the three major ingredients. Many growers use nothing but a standard liquid fertilizer with excellent results. A *tomato-type liquid fertilizer* is formulated specially for use with tomato plants, encouraging them to produce lots of flowers and fruit of good colour and shape. It contains a higher proportion of potassium than other fertilizers and is very useful for flowering and fruiting (berrying) plants indoors.

Capillary matting *To water your plants while you are away, stand them on a piece of capillary matting on the draining board. Hang one end of the matting in the sink and partially fill this with water. Moisture will be taken up from the capillary matting into the potting mixture by capillary action.*

Temporary wick *Another method of self-watering is to use a wick. Place one end in water and the other in the potting mixture. Water will be absorbed by capillary action.*

THE RIGHT QUANTITY OF WATER

Watering sparingly
Water a plant when two-thirds of the mixture is dry (1). Barely cover the surface of the mixture with water (2). Test the mixture with a thin stake. If there are dry patches, add more water (3).

Watering moderately
Water a plant when the top 1-2 cm ($\frac{1}{2}$ in) of the mixture feels dry (1). Pour water on to the mixture until it is thoroughly moist (2). Stop watering when water appears in the saucer (3).

Watering plentifully
Water a plant when the surface of the mixture feels dry (1). Flood the surface with water until the mixture is saturated (2). When the excess water has drained away, empty the saucer (3).

Potting and Repotting

Within the confines of their pots house plants have a very restricted root run compared with garden or wild plants. Young actively-growing plants grow surprisingly quickly; they soon fill their pots with roots and exhaust the nutrients in the potting mixture. The solution is to repot them into a larger pot or to provide them with fresh mixture in the same-sized pot.

Potting mixtures

There are basically two types of potting mixture: soil-based and peat-based. Soil-based mixtures contain a large proportion of loam with peat and sand added. The loam contains a quantity of nutrients that are available for the plant to draw on and these often last up to a year. Soil-based potting mixtures are heavy and suitable for large plants. Peat-based potting mixtures contain very little nutrients, but they are lighter and cleaner to handle than soil-based ones. Both types of potting mixture have fertilizer added to them. Do not be tempted to use garden soil for growing house plants as this contains harmful things, such as pests, fungus disease spores and weed seeds.

There are other elements that can be added to potting mixtures to help let in air, assist with drainage or help it to retain more moisture. Coarse sand and grit, chunky pieces of peat, leafmould or bark chippings and perlite (expanded volcanic rock) all open up the mixture. Other ingredients such as fine peat, sphagnum moss and vermiculite hold moisture in the mixture.

Each type of potting mixture has its advantages; many growers use one as a base and add to it the ingredients that help to improve it for individual plants.

Potting

Potting means literally putting a plant into a pot. The plant can be a small seedling, a single cutting, or a collection of rooted cuttings. Small pots should be used at this stage because roots are not extensive, and in a large pot much of the potting mixture would be wasted. If potting the plant in a clay pot, it is best to insert a piece of broken pot (called a shard) inside the pot, covering the single drainage hole. This will prevent the mixture being washed out of the pot. You can also add some extra coarse-textured material, such as gravel or small stones, at the bottom of the pot. This will help to improve drainage. Plastic pots do not normally need any material at the base of the pot.

Partially fill the pot with a suitable potting mixture. Then hold the small plantlet or cutting to be potted just above the mixture, so that its sparse roots touch the mixture, and its crown is just below the rim of the pot, and then fill the pot almost to the top, so that the roots are buried. Always leave enough space at the top of the pot for subsequent waterings. If the pot is filled too full, this makes it difficult to apply enough water in one application to satisfy the plant, which may result in the plant going short of water. Firm the mixture down gently with fingers or thumbs.

Repotting

Repotting is necessary when a plant needs new potting mixture to grow into. This is either when the plant outgrows its pot, or the potting mixture is spent. Repotting should be done at the beginning of spring. Many plants do not need a bigger root run; they are content with what they have, but require fresh potting mixture to live on. These plants require repotting in a pot of the same size. First take the plant out of the pot, and then remove most of the old spent potting mixture, being careful not to damage the roots. Then return the plant to a clean pot of the same size and top it up with fresh potting mixture.

Repotting a plant into a larger pot allows the plant to grow to greater stature or to reach maturity. It is important not to give a plant too large a pot; you should only

POTTING A PLANT

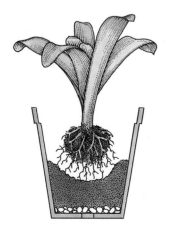

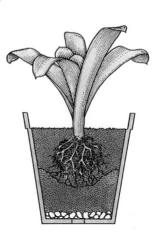

1 Insert a layer of coarse-textured material, such as small stones or grit, in the pot, then add a layer of potting mixture. Suspend the plant over the mixture to check that its crown will be just below the rim of the pot.

2 Lower the plant into the pot so that its roots touch the potting mixture, and its crown is just below the rim of the pot. Then fill the pot almost to the top with potting mixture and firm it down gently.

1

2

move a plant on into the next size pot or two sizes larger at the maximum. To repot a plant in a bigger pot, first prepare the larger pot by placing some potting mixture on the bottom. Ensure that the plant will be positioned in its new pot at the same level that it had in the old pot. You can do this by making a mould (see the illustration, right) and then slipping the rootball of the plant into the moulded shape. This method of repotting has great advantages in that it cuts out much of the mess that can be incurred and causes very little damage to the plant.

Topdressing

When a plant reaches its maximum practical pot size there is only really one solution to the problem of providing it with its extra nourishment. This is topdressing and involves carefully scraping away a few centimetres of the old mixture from the top of the pot, being careful to avoid damaging the plant's roots, and then topping up with fresh, rich (usually soil-based) potting mixture.

Making a mould *An efficient way of repotting is to put the old pot into the new one, and fill the gap between the two with potting mixture. Then remove the inner pot and insert the plant into the mould shape.*

Pruning the rootball *When repotting a plant into the same size pot, you may need to prune the roots to allow room for the new potting mixture. To do this, cut a slice off the bottom or each side with a sharp knife.*

TOPDRESSING

1 Using a fork, carefully scrape away the top layer of the potting mixture.

2 Refill the pot to its original level with fresh potting mixture and firm it in.

REPOTTING A PLANT

1 Place one hand on the mixture, keeping the stem between your fingers.

2 Turn the pot upside-down and gently tap it on the edge of a table.

3 The plant and its rootball should then slide out into your hand.

4 Remove any moss or other green growth from the top of the mixture.

5 Put a layer of grit in a larger-sized pot, then position the plant.

6 Fill in the gaps around the rootball with potting mixture and firm in.

Simple Propagation

In time all house plants grow too big or pass their prime and are best replaced with younger, more vigorous plants. This can easily be done by propagating your own plants. The two main ways are growing new plants from seed (which can be a slow and haphazard process, resulting in far too many plants or worse, none at all) and by taking off pieces of a plant and inducing them to grow roots of their own. This is called vegetative propagation. Virtually any part of a plant can be used for propagation: leaves, stems, offsets, or the plant can be divided at the roots. Usually each plant responds well to only one particular method, but sometimes you have a choice.

The best season for most methods of propagation is the spring and early summer when temperatures are warm and when there is plenty of light.

Stem cuttings

This method involves cutting off a short piece of the stem and then rooting it. Most house plants can be propagated in this way, whether they have soft stems or hard, woody stems. The best section of stem to use is the tip of a shoot, and this is called a tip cutting. Other sections of the stem can be used as cuttings, but these will take longer to root than a tip cutting. Stem cuttings will root either in rooting mixture made up of equal parts of peat and coarse sand or perlite, or in water. Rooting mixture differs from potting mixture in that it is very low in fertilizer, thus encouraging roots to grow in search of food.

To encourage a cutting to root, place a plastic dome or plastic bag over it. This will keep the cutting warm and provide a humid atmosphere, encouraging the roots to grow. If using a plastic bag, prop it up with short canes pushed into the potting mixture to keep it out of direct contact with the cuttings. Stand the cutting in a warm position in bright filtered light. Some plants, such as pelargoniums, prefer not to have a humid atmosphere and are best rooted uncovered.

Some cuttings root surprisingly quickly, while others take longer; much depends on both the individual plant and the temperature. Rooting is normally said to have occurred when strong new growth begins at the tip of the cutting. When the cutting is well established, transplant it into a suitable potting mixture.

Leaf cuttings

This method of propagation is used most frequently with African violets (*Saintpaulia* hybrids), some begonias, and many succulents. In the case of the succulents it is a simple matter of placing the single leaves on a layer of moist sand. New tiny plantlets will then form at the ends of the leaves where they were attached to the plant. Pot these when they are large enough to handle.

SOFT STEM CUTTING

1 Make a clean cut just above a leaf. This encourages the parent plant to develop new shoots.

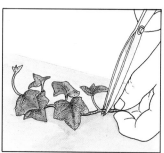

2 Trim the cutting immediately below the lowest leaf node and remove the lower leaves.

3a *Either* root the cutting in water and pot it up when its roots have grown to 2–4 cm (1–1½ in) long.

3b *Or* plant the cutting directly in rooting mixture and cover it with a plastic bag to conserve humidity.

WOODY STEM CUTTING

1 Remove any lower leaves from the stem. Cut the stem into short pieces, each of which should include at least one node.

2 Place the stem cuttings either vertically or horizontally (it does not matter which) in the rooting mixture. Roots will then grow from buried nodes, whilst shoots will develop from nodes exposed to the air.

In the case of African violets and begonias, place the leaf in barely moist rooting mixture at an angle of 45 degrees, cover it with a plastic bag, and keep it in bright light until new roots develop. When it is possible to handle the individual plantlets, separate them from the cluster that usually forms and then pot them individually into small pots filled with potting mixture. Leaf cuttings can also be rooted initially in water and then transferred into potting mixture after the roots have formed.

Rooting plantlets

Some plants produce small replicas of themselves on their leaves or on trailing stems or stolons (see page 142). These often have some roots already formed so they can be detached and potted, but if not they quickly grow roots when placed in contact with a suitable rooting medium. Plants that develop in this way include *Chlorophytum comosum, Saxifraga stolonifera, Tolmiea menziesii* and *Asplenium bulbiferum*.

Rooting offsets

Offsets are small plants that form around the base of the parent plant. Bromeliads and most cacti are examples of plants that produce offsets. Before propagating by this method, the offsets should be well developed. First detach the offset from the parent plant. Sometimes these can simply be pulled off the parent plant; in other cases you may need a sharp knife to separate them. Most offsets will already have some roots attached to them and they simply require potting up in small pots filled with potting mixture. Water sparingly until they are well established.

Dividing plants

Some plants, such as most ferns and some cacti, develop dense clumps of growth that can easily be divided to produce new plants. Simply remove the plant from its pot and gently pull sections apart, ensuring that each has a well-developed cluster of growing stems and some roots attached. Pot up each section of the plant in a separate pot of potting mixture. If there are plenty of roots the sections will grow away quickly and not need any special attention. If there are only a few roots, cover the pot with a plastic dome or bag for a week or two to conserve moisture until growth is established.

ROOTING A LEAF CUTTING

1 Remove a single leaf from the plant with a sharp knife. Then trim the leaf stalk to a length of around 4-5 cm (2 in).

2 Make a hole in the rooting mixture with a pencil or finger and then plant the leaf at an angle of 45 degrees.

3 Cover the pot with a plastic bag or rigid plastic dome to increase the humidity, and keep it in bright filtered light.

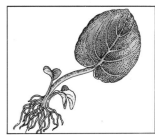

4 Roots will develop in about five to six weeks and soon after small plantlets will grow. Cut away the parent leaf.

ROOTING PLANTLETS

1 Cut off a leaf or stolon bearing a plantlet. Leave about 3 cm (1½ in) of the stalk or stolon attached and then bury this in rooting mixture, so that the plantlet rests on the surface.

2 Cover the pot with a plastic bag or rigid plastic dome to conserve humidity during the rooting process. Stand the pot in bright filtered light to keep the plantlet warm. Roots will develop in a few weeks.

DIVIDING PLANTS

1 Remove the plant from its pot and gently pull the sections of the plant apart, ensuring that each section has a well developed and healthy cluster of growing stems and some roots attached.

2 Pot up each section of the plant in a separate pot. If there are only a few roots, cover each pot with a plastic bag or dome for a week or two to conserve humidity until new growth appears.

Trouble-Shooting Guide

CULTURAL PROBLEMS

When a plant looks unhealthy, in most cases pests and diseases are not to blame. It is usually poor growing conditions, neglect or the wrong treatment that cause the problems. These faults can be corrected, if diagnosed accurately, and the plant will usually recover and resume healthy growth. To help you diagnose the faults, a diagram showing the most common cultural problems from which house plants can suffer is illustrated below.

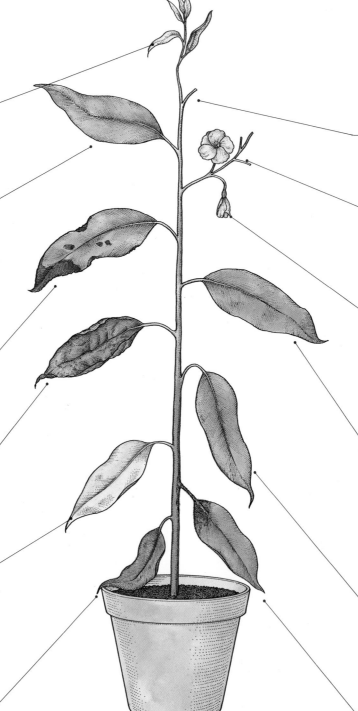

Elongated growth, pale leaves and stems
This is usually a sign of lack of light. Cut back the leggy stems to encourage bushy growth, and move the plant to a brighter position.

Variegated leaves turn green
When variegated leaves turn green, it is because of poor light. Move the plant to a more brightly lit position.

Brown patches on leaves
This can be caused by sun scorch, which can occur when plants are suddenly placed in strong sunlight. Cut out the scorched sections and leave the plant to outgrow any disfigurement. Always accustom plants to brighter light very gradually.

Curled leaf edges
This is often an indication of the plant receiving too bright a light. Move the plant to a shadier position.

Leaves turn yellow and fall
When several leaves turn yellow and fall at the same time, the plant is probably in a draught. Check that the plant is not standing by a half-opened window.

Lower leaves dry up and fall
The plant may be getting too little light, too much heat or not enough water. Move the plant to a brighter position, away from any obvious source of heat, such as a radiator, and make sure it is given enough water.

Leaf fall
A sudden leaf fall is usually due to a shock to the plant's system, for example a sudden drop in temperature, a cold draught or dryness at the roots. Move the plant to a sheltered position and make sure it has enough water.

Lack of flowers
This might be an indication of poor light. Move the plant to a brighter position.

Flowers quickly drop
This often occurs when the temperature is too high for the plant. High humidity will counteract this, so stand the pot on a tray of moist pebbles.

Brown leaf tips and margins
This is usually a result of dry air, and is likely to occur on plants with thin leaves. To counteract this, stand the pot on a tray of moist pebbles and mist-spray frequently.

Wilting leaves
If the potting mixture is dry, the plant is short of water. Soak the pot in a bowl of water for half an hour to revive it. If, however, the potting mixture is very wet, the plant is suffering from overwatering. Repot into barely moist potting mixture.

Rotting stems and leaves
This is an attack of disease that often occurs when the plant has poor growing conditions. Remove the damaged leaves and make sure the plant is not being overwatered.

PESTS

It is wise to examine your plants frequently for possible signs of pests and to take prompt action with the first arrivals. Most pests have a very high mortality rate and reproduce rapidly to compensate for natural losses. Some pests only attack certain plants; others are less discriminating. Minor attacks of pests are hardly noticeable on a plant but it is at this stage that they can best be dealt with. Either pick off the odd, stray pest, or give the plant a soapy water wash. If the problem has gone beyond that stage then you must resort to chemical insecticides.

Insecticides fall into two broad groups: systemic insecticides and contact insecticides. Systemic insecticides contain chemicals that are absorbed by the leaves or are taken up by the roots. They poison the leaves or sap and thus kill leaf-eating and sap-sucking pests but do not harm the plant. Contact insecticides are sprayed directly on to the insects, killing them on contact, either by affecting their respiratory systems, or otherwise destroying them. Insecticides are available as aerosols, dusts, liquids, granules, and sprays.

APHIDS (Greenflies and blackflies)

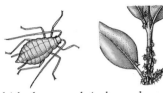

Aphids that attack indoor plants are usually green. They grow and multiply rapidly, frequently casting off old white skin cases as they grow. Aphids live by sucking sap from plants, which causes distortion of the leaves, stems and flowers. They exude quantities of sugars, causing sticky patches on leaves (and on furniture) on which sooty mould can grow. They can also pass on diseases and viruses from one plant to another. Most plants, except those with leathery leaves, are susceptible to attack from aphids. Heavy mist-spraying with water will often dislodge a small colony but it is important to keep up the attack for a while as the tiny offspring can go undetected for some days. Use a contact spray such as liquid derris or a systemic insecticide if the attack is severe.

CATERPILLARS

Caterpillars are the larval stage of butterflies and moths. The most common caterpillar to attack house plants is that of the tortrix moth. This caterpillar spins fine silken webs that are used to draw leaves, flowers or stems together, thus providing a hiding place for the caterpillar to feed on the leaves and young shoots. To deal with this pest saturate the plant with a contact spray such as liquid derris, or a systemic insecticide.

EARTHWORMS

Earthworms are a nuisance to indoor plants, as their constant burrowing loosens the potting mixture and can disturb roots. Apply a solution of permanganate of potash to the potting mixture, and this will send the worms hurrying to the surface, where they can be picked off and disposed of.

FUNGUS GNATS

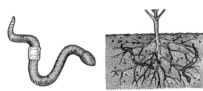

These are also known as sciarid or mushroom flies. They fly rather sluggishly over the potting mixture and are more irritating than harmful. Their larvae are not normally visible as they feed on decaying matter in the potting mixture. They do no real harm to strong-growing plants but can harm small seedlings or plantlets. They can become active in any peat-based potting mixture. A systemic insecticide used as a drench will dispose of them effectively.

MEALY BUGS AND ROOT MEALY BUGS

Mealy bugs look like tiny, white woodlice. They are covered with a white mealy wax that water cannot penetrate. They collect in small colonies on a plant, particularly in leaf axils, the crowns and at leaf bases. They suck up sap and exude surplus sugary matter. They are very difficult to eradicate. Tight-growing, rosette-shaped plants such as aeoniums and saintpaulias are susceptible. Root mealy bugs are very similar, but they feed on the roots of plants. Cacti and succulents are most prone to attack.

To treat an attack drench the potting mixture with a systemic insecticide, but do not use this method on ferns or cacti. Alternatively, dab the stray mealy bugs found lurking between leaves with a small swab dipped in diluted methylated spirit. A deterrent for root mealy bugs is to incorporate gamma HCH dust into the potting mixture when repotting.

RED SPIDER MITES

These pests feed and breed on the undersides of the leaves. They are barely visible to the naked eye, but can be detected by the webs that they spin between leaves and particularly around leaf axils. They also suck sap from the leaves, causing unsightly mottling on the upper surface of the leaves. In severe cases, they can cause new growth to become stunted, and leaves to fall. These mites are often called greenhouse red spider mites as they thrive under cover, in hot dry air. A humid atmosphere (which is what many house plants prefer) and frequent mist-spraying, aimed particularly at the leaf undersides, will discourage an attack from taking place and certainly reduce the number of mites considerably. An attack caught in good time can often be totally eliminated with frequent spraying of water over a week or two. To treat a more serious attack, spray the plant weekly with liquid derris, directing the spray on to both the upper and lower surfaces of the leaves, or drench the potting mixture with a systemic insecticide.

SCALE INSECTS

Scale insects are brown or yellowish in colour; they congregate near to the midribs and raised areas on the undersides of leaves. They suck sap,

exude a sticky substance and are difficult to eradicate completely. Often the first sign of their presence is a sticky residue noticeable on the leaves, or on furniture. The young insects are very active, but the mature females are immobile. Under their protective hard shells they lay eggs and when the young (aptly called crawlers) hatch, they creep away to find a suitable permanent site for themselves to start feeding. The best way to treat this pest is to use a systemic insecticide.

VINE WEEVILS

This pest is troublesome at all stages of its life. The adult weevil is large and coloured black with six legs and a distinct snout; it eats pieces out of leaf edges, causing disfiguration. The cream-coloured grubs live in the potting mixture where they systematically set about eating the roots, tubers or underground stems of plants. They can eventually eat up everything below the surface of the potting mixture, and leave a limp, rootless plant sitting on the surface. The weevil favours low-growing rosette-shaped plants for its grubs,

laying its eggs in the potting mixture and then moving on to fresh plants. Echeverias, aloes, many other succulents, rhizomatous begonias, primulas, cyclamens and saintpaulias can all be attacked. To treat this pest drench the potting mixture with a systemic insecticide and incorporate gamma HCH dust in new potting mixture at the time of potting or repotting a plant.

WHITEFLIES

Whiteflies are tiny, moth-like creatures. They have three stages of growth: eggs, nymphs and adults. The nymphs and adults cause the damage. They settle mainly on the undersides of leaves, suck sap from the plant and exude sticky honeydew, on which sooty mould can grow. They also cause tiny pits on the leaves and flowers. They are very active, and fly short distances if disturbed. They lay their eggs in large numbers on the leaf undersides. Use a systemic insecticide to deal with this pest; as eggs are unaffected by insecticides, any application may have to be repeated several times, to allow the eggs time to mature.

DISEASES

The best way to prevent disease is to give plants good growing conditions. House plants suffer from very few diseases and those that they may get are usually as a result of unsuitable growing conditions that allow fungi and bacteria to develop and then spread. If a plant appears to be ailing, check in the A-Z Plant Guide that you are providing the right amount of light, water and heat and the correct level of humidity. Check also that the pot size is right and that you are using the correct type of potting mixture. An overwet potting mixture, poor circulation of air or air that is cool and highly charged with moisture are usually contributory factors. Many pests transmit diseases, as well as weakening a plant and making it more susceptible to disease.

Keep a careful check on your plants. Always remove damaged sections, such as bruised stems or broken leaves, as soon as you see them, since they are susceptible to rot, as are cuttings in the process of rooting. Cut away any damaged tissue with a clean, sharp knife, allow the wound to dry and then dust it with fungicidal powder. If you discover a diseased cutting growing with several other healthy ones, remove it immediately before the disease can spread. It is a good idea to use a sterile potting mixture as this minimizes the risk of disease attacking roots. It is also advisable to remove any fallen leaves and flowers as soon as you spot them to prevent them from decaying on the potting mixture. If a plant becomes so badly affected that it cannot be cured, it is best to throw it away.

BLACKLEG

This disease is limited to just one popular house plant, the otherwise very easy pelargonium. It usually occurs as a result of overwatering. It strikes the plant at the point where the stem enters the potting mixture and it gradually creeps both upwards and downwards. The stem goes black, a disintegration that looks like withering occurs and quite soon the stem keels over. The disease is particularly liable to attack pelargonium cuttings that are being rooted, as the raw edge of the cut stem section is especially vulnerable. To avoid this problem, make sure that the rooting mixture is kept only barely moist, that the stem sits on and in a little area of coarse sand or grit (to ensure that the mixture touching the stem is well drained) and that the cutting is not covered with a plastic covering. Water the cutting very sparingly until it has developed roots and avoid knocking the stems. Should the disease strike, cut away the damaged section and dust any remaining sound section with green sulphur dust.

GREY MOULD (Botrytis)

Grey mould is a fungus that attacks dead and decaying plant tissue and it can start when a stem or leaf is injured. Spores of the fungus are always present in the air, and they can spread rapidly to live, healthy tissue. Infection can also start when faded flowers and leaves fall off plants on to moist potting mixture and start to decay. The mould usually attacks when air is damp and still, and when the temperature is low, rarely during the warmer summer months and when there is good ventilation. Plants with soft stems and leaves, such as saintpaulias and cinerarias, are particularly susceptible to grey mould. An infection on saintpaulias can start if moisture lodges for any time in the crown of the plant, or if broken sections of leaf stalk or flower stalk are left in the heart of the plant. A badly infected section looks like an unpleasant mound of fluffy grey mould. One way to treat an infected plant is to dab green sulphur dust on to the injured sections, or spray the plant with a fungicide containing benomyl.

SOOTY MOULD

Sooty mould is a fungus that lives on the honeydew secreted by aphids and other sucking insects. It looks like a thin layer of soot and is unpleasant to touch. Although it does no real harm to the leaves or stems, it does, however, prevent light from reaching the leaves and blocks the breathing pores (stomata). Shrubs of the citrus family, including *Citrofortunella mitis* and *Pentas lanceolata* are very susceptible. To deal with sooty mould, use soapy water to wash off the black deposit but tackle the *real* problem, the sap-sucking insects, with a suitable insecticide.

MILDEW (Powdery mildew)

Mildew appears on the surface of leaves and stems and is first apparent as tiny patches of white mould. It can be distinguished from grey mould by the lack of fluffy growths. If you wipe these away with a finger, you will see a dark patch remaining on the plant tissue beneath, which indicates injury. Quite large patches of mildew can develop and cause distortion and leaf fall. Mildew is encouraged by a humid atmosphere, poor ventilation, sudden low temperatures, or erratic watering. Some begonias, particularly *Begonia sutherlandii,* can be susceptible, and soft-leaved plants in general are prone to attack. To treat an attack of mildew, pick off all affected leaves, and spray the plant with a systemic fungicide containing bupirimate and triforine. This will prevent further spread of the powdery white markings but the damaged tissue will remain as darker stains.

STEM, ROOT AND CROWN ROT

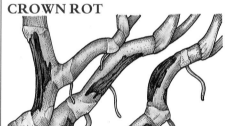

When a stem is attacked by this fungal disease, it turns soft and slimy. Rot can attack very soft-stemmed plants, such as *Impatiens wallerana* or *Exacum affine,* but also globular or columnar cacti, and the thicker stems of philodendrons and their relatives. To treat stem rot, cut out the infected sections, dust the wounds with powdered sulphur and keep the plant much drier at the roots. Fungicides can be effective if the infection is caught in time.

Root rot causes the roots to become soft and slimy. It is due to over-watering and there seems to be no cure.

Crown rot is usually caused by allowing water to lodge in the heart of a plant, particularly rosette-shaped plants, such as *Saintpaulia* hybrids. It causes the leaves to turn soft and soggy and this then spreads outwards. Always remove any fallen flowers, leaf stalks and flower stalks right down to their bases. To treat crown rot, cut out the damaged sections and spray with a fungicide.

Glossary

Active growth period The time when a plant is developing new growth.

Aerial roots Roots that grow from a plant's stems to take nutrients from the air or to cling to surfaces.

Areole Unique to the cactus family, this is a section of the stem from which grow hairs, spines, and flowers.

Axil The point between the leaf stalk and stem from which new growth or a flowerbud develops.

Blade The main part of the leaf.

Bloom A delicate powdery or waxy coating to a leaf or fruit.

Bog plant A plant that grows on wet spongy ground.

Bract A modified leaf, frequently backing or surrounding a flower or cluster of flowers. It is often highly coloured to attract pollinating insects.

Bud An immature leaf or flower that is often protected by hard scales.

Bulbil An immature bulb, that may grow from the base of the "parent" bulb in the potting mixture.

Capillary action The drawing up of water by, for example, potting mixture when the pot is in contact with water.

Crown The area at the base or centre of a plant from which shoots and roots grow.

Cutting A section of a stem or leaf that is used in propagation.

Division Separating sections of the *rootball* with plenty of top growth, for use in propagation.

Dormancy, dormant period See *Rest period*.

Double flower A flower that has two or more layers of petals.

Epiphyte A plant that grows on another plant, for example many bromeliads and ferns. It takes food and water from the atmosphere and from plant debris that may have collected among the branches of the host plant.

Flower-head, flower spike A flower or collection of flowers that has many components, often including bracts.

Foliage plant A plant that is grown for its leaves.

Frond The name used to describe a fern or palm leaf.

Fungicide A chemical used to prevent or tackle fungus disease.

Glochid A small bristle or bristly patch found on the areoles of some cacti.

Growing point The tip of a shoot from which new growth develops.

Hardy Able to withstand frost.

Hybrid A plant developed by crossing two different species.

Insecticide A chemical used to combat insects and other pests.

Latex A sticky, white sap that flows from certain plants when they are cut.

Leaf cutting A leaf, usually with stalk attached, that is used in propagation.

Leaflet A small section of any leaf that is divided into sections.

Leafmould Partially rotted leaves used in potting mixture to help retain moisture whilst also allowing air into the mixture.

Leggy Elongated growth, usually caused by insufficient light.

Margin The edge of a leaf or flower. This may be a different colour to the main body of the leaf or flower.

Midrib The main vein of a leaf. It is often stout and raised.

Moss pole A pole or cylinder covered or filled with moist moss, that is used as a plant support. The moist moss encourages *aerial roots* to develop on the plant and grow into the moss pole.

Node A joint or swelling, usually on the opposite side of the stem to a leaf axil, from which roots develop when a section of stem is used in propagation.

Offset A small plant that develops, usually at the base of a plant, and can be used in propagation.

Perlite Expanded volcanic rock used in potting mixture to give it an open free-draining texture.

Photosynthesis The process by which the plant uses water, air and light to manufacture much of its own food.

Pinching out, nipping out Removing a soft shoot with thumb and forefinger to encourage side-shoots to develop.

Plantlet A young plant. Often used to describe "offspring" that are produced on leaves or stolons.

Pot-bound A plant that has filled its pot with roots and is in need of repotting into a bigger pot.

Rest period A time usually during the winter, when a plant stops growing and takes a rest.

Rhizome A usually horizontal stem, sometimes underground, from which new growth is produced. A rhizome is capable of storing food and water for use during dry periods.

Rootball The mass of potting mixture and roots that is seen when a plant is taken out of its pot.

Rosette A circular arrangement of leaves around a *crown* or the centre of the plant.

Runner A thin stem that can root into potting mixture and develop a new plant.

Scurf Scales on a leaf, often giving it a grey appearance.

Semi-double flower A flower that has more than a single layer of petals, but not quite two layers.

Single flower A flower that has a single layer of petals.

Spathe A showy modified bract forming part of the flower-head of some plants, such as anthurium.

Sphagnum moss Moss that holds a large quantity of water, yet admits lots of air. It is used in some potting mixtures and for filling a moss pole.

Spore The minute reproductive body of a fern. Spores are stored in spore cases that are visible underneath some fern fronds.

Stem cutting A section of a plant's stem used in propagation.

Stolon A creeping stem that grows new plants at its tip.

Succulent A plant capable of withstanding periods of water shortage. Also used to describe a very fleshy leaf.

Sucker A shoot that appears from beneath the potting mixture, growing either from the root, or from the part of the stem that is buried. It makes leaves and roots of its own.

Systemic A form of insecticide or fungicide that is applied to the leaves or roots of a plant and enters the system (sap and tissue) of the plant.

Temporary house plant A plant that is displayed only on a temporary basis. It might be an annual or one that is treated as an annual, because it is too difficult to keep for another year, or because it has a long, dull period between flushes of blooming.

Tendril A thin growth from the stem or leaf that can wind itself round a nearby support, enabling a plant to climb.

Terrestrial A plant that grows in the ground. The term is used particularly of bromeliads.

Topdressing The action of scraping away the top layer of potting mixture and replacing it with fresh mixture. A plant is topdressed when it has grown too big to repot into a larger pot.

Tuber A fleshy or hard storage organ, often growing underground, that enables the plant to overwinter.

Variegated A leaf or flower that has spots, streaks or other markings of a different colour.

Vein A strand of thicker tissue in a leaf that is used to distribute water and nutrients. It is often raised or a different colour from the rest of the leaf.

Woody A stem that has developed a hard outer coating.

Index

Acknowledgments

Author's acknowledgments
I should like to thank the following: Heather Dewhurst for editing the book, for her quick grasp of what I had intended and for reducing my manuscript down to essentials; and Fiona Macmillan who gave so much thought to the layout and presented it so handsomely. I very much enjoyed working with them both. I would also like to thank Gwen Goodship who gave me advice on the latest and "safest" chemicals to tackle the problems that house plants (and we growers) have to face.

Over the years house plants have given me great pleasure and I would like to thank whoever it was for first pointing me in their direction.

Dorling Kindersley would like to thank the following for their help in supplying plants and props: Des Whitwell of Chessington Nurseries Ltd, Joan Clifton of Clifton Nurseries Ltd, Terry Hewitt of Holly Gate Cactus Nursery, Ron Lucibell, Barbara Potter, Syon Park Garden Centre, and Ray Waite of RHS Garden, Wisley.

And the following for kindly letting us photograph their homes: Roger Bristow, Jackie Douglas, Sue Dyer, Jenny Engelmann, and Letty Macmillan.

Finally, the following for their help in the production of this book: Simon Adams, Sandra Archer, Hilary Bird, Chambers Wallace, Kate Grant, Mark Kebell, Sarah Kellaghan, and Judy Sandeman.

Photographic credits
All photography by Geoff Dann except for:
Michael Boys: 8, 9
Eric Crichton: 51L, 89C
Dave King: 5, 20, 22L, 23, 24L, 28L, 29, 30B, 32T, 36L, 39L, 40C, 41L, 42, 43, 45, 46L, 46C, 48L, 49L, 49C, 50R, 52, 53L, 55, 56R, 58L, 59B, 60, 61R, 64L, 65C, 66, 67L, 68R, 69, 71, 72L, 73, 74R, 75B, 78, 79, 80C, 81R, 82C, 86, 87, 88R, 89L, 90R, 92, 95, 96C, 98L, 99C, 99R, 101R, 102, 103, 104, 105R, 106R, 109R, 114R, 115, 116R, 118R, 119, 120
Harry Smith Horticultural Photographic Collection: 99L, 109L

T = top, B = bottom, L = left, R = right, C = centre

Illustrators
David Ashby, Will Giles, Vana Haggerty, Vanessa Luff, and Sandra Pond.

READING SUCCESS
WITH COSY & CUDDLE

LOST IN WOOLLY WOOD

Written by Elizabeth Taylor
Illustrated by Colin Petty

 Children's Leisure Products Ltd.

One day, Cosy was telling Cuddle about mysteries.

It was a rainy day, and Cosy and Cuddle were staying indoors. Cosy Bear was telling Cuddle about mysteries. "A mystery is something no one understands," explained Cosy Bear. "Like when I open the biscuit tin and find it's empty. Only that's not a proper mystery because I know you ate all the biscuits. A mystery is something you have to solve."

The next day the sun was shining again. Cuddle decided to go exploring, and look for a mystery. He had only just opened his garden gate when he saw a piece of pink string. "Whose string is this?" he wondered. He thought hard, but he didn't know. "This must be a mystery," he said happily.

Cuddle decided to look for a mystery. He saw a piece of string.

He rolled the string into a ball.

Cuddle followed the string, rolling it into a ball as he went. He rolled it all the way to Mrs Rabbit's house. It was bath day, and Mrs Rabbit was outside washing Teeny and Tiny in a tub. They were shouting and laughing and splashing soap suds everywhere.

"Is this your string?" shouted Cuddle above all the noise.

It wasn't Mrs Rabbit's string.

"Come closer," shouted Mrs Rabbit. "I can't hear."

"Is this your string?" Cuddle asked again when he was nearer.

Teeny and Tiny waited until Cuddle was right beside them, then SPLASH! They soaked him with bubble bath!

Mrs Rabbit laughed. "It's not my string," she said.

The string led to Mr Mole's house.

The string led into Woolly Wood. Cuddle followed it to Mr Mole's house. He knew it was Mr Mole's house because by the side of the path he saw a pile of soil. Then he saw another, and another. Mr Mole was *always* moving house.

"Mr Mole!" he called at the first pile. There was no answer, so he tried another pile. "Mr Mole!"

He was about to give up when Mr Mole popped up right behind him. "Cooee," he called. "It's no good looking for me over there. That's where I was yesterday."

"Why can't you live in one place like other people?" laughed Cuddle. Then he remembered the string. "Is this yours?" he asked.

Mr Mole looked at it very carefully. "No, it's not my string," he said. "It's a mystery!"

It wasn't Mr Mole's string.

Cuddle found another piece of string.

Cuddle was beginning to wonder if he would ever solve the mystery — when he saw *another* piece of string. It was blue, and it was hanging from the tree where Mrs Tweet lived. Cuddle tingled from nose to tail with excitement.

"I wonder if it joins up with my pink string?" he said.

He tugged at it carefully, then he tugged it a bit harder. Suddenly, something large and wet landed right on top of him! He had been pulling Mrs Tweet's washing line, and he had pulled it right off the tree! Mrs Tweet flew down, flapping her wings crossly.

It was Mrs Tweet's washing line.

Cuddle had not solved the mystery.

"I am sorry," said Cuddle, holding up the pink ball of string. "I thought this might be yours."

"No, it is not," said Mrs Tweet. "And I would be glad if you would leave my *blue* string alone!"

Cuddle helped Mrs Tweet hang up the washing again. "I wonder if solving mysteries is always this troublesome," he thought.

Waving Mrs Tweet goodbye, he set off once more. The string led deeper and deeper into Woolly Wood.

Very soon the string was almost too big to carry, and it was very heavy. "It's getting dark, too," thought Cuddle, peering into the gloomy wood around him. He decided to keep walking until he had counted to a hundred. "If I haven't solved the mystery by then, I'll go home," he told himself. He counted his steps. "One, two, three . . ."

It was getting dark.

Suddenly he bumped into Cosy Bear.

"... eighty-eight, eighty-nine ..." Cuddle was so busy watching his feet — because it helped him to count — that he did not look where he was going. "Ninety, ninety-one ..." Bump!

He walked right into Cosy Bear!

Cosy was cross.

"What are you doing?" asked Cosy.

"Oh, it's you," said Cuddle. "I'm out to solve the mystery of the string."

"It's no mystery. That's my string," said Cosy Bear, crossly.

"The string was to show me the way home," said Cosy.

"Why did you leave it lying on the ground?" asked Cuddle, puzzled.

"The string was to show me the way home," said Cosy. "Now you've rolled it up — I'm lost!"

"Don't worry," said Cuddle. "I'll unroll the string exactly as I rolled it up . . . we'll easily find our way back."

Cuddle started to unroll the string. "Now, did I come this way . . . or from over there?" he wondered.

"I think this way's home," called Cosy Bear, pointing in a different direction.

But it was no good. They were lost in Woolly Wood. They walked for what seemed like miles until they got too tired to go any further.

Cosy and Cuddle were lost.

They decided to sleep in the wood and find their way home in the morning. They found a sheltered hollow beneath a giant tree and that night they slept on a bed of leaves.

"Cosy Bear," said Cuddle sleepily, as he snuggled down. "Why did you come to Woolly Wood?"

"I wanted to find a very rare and lovely flower that only grows here," explained Cosy Bear.

But before he could say any more, Cuddle fell fast asleep.

They slept on a bed of leaves.

In the morning Cosy saw a lovely flower.

The leaves kept them dry and warm and they slept soundly all night long. In the morning Cosy woke up first. He rubbed his eyes very hard as though he couldn't believe what he saw. "Cuddle! Wake up!" he shouted. "We've found it!"

"Found what?" yawned Cuddle.

"We've found the rare flower I was looking for!" said Cosy.

Cosy collected some flower seeds.

When Cosy and Cuddle had scooped up the leaves to make their bed they had uncovered the flower. It had been hidden under the leaves all the time. Cosy collected some flower seeds that were lying on the ground, to plant in his garden.

"Isn't the flower beautiful?" said Cosy.

"Oh, come on," said Cuddle. "Let's find our way home. I want some breakfast!"

They started to argue about which way to go, when Cosy Bear suddenly cried out, "Look!" It was Cosy Bear's garden gate, right in front of them. Cosy and Cuddle had found their way home. In the dark they had walked to the very edge of the wood, and fallen asleep just a few steps from Cosy Bear's house!

Cosy and Cuddle found their way home.

When summer came Cosy's seeds grew into lovely flowers. It was a happy ending to the mystery.

"I'm glad you rolled up the string," said Cosy, happily. "If you hadn't got us lost I might never have found my rare and lovely flower."

"Hmm," said Cuddle, who wasn't sure he liked sleeping under piles of leaves. "Next time I find a mystery I think I'll just let it be mysterious!"

The seeds grew into lovely flowers. It was a happy ending to the mystery.